Chinchillas

Project Team
Editor: Mary E. Grangeia
Copy Editor: Stephanie Fornino
Interior Design: Leah Lococo Ltd. and Stephanie Krautheim
Design Layout: Stephanie Krautheim
Cover Design Angela Stanford

United Kingdom Editorial Team
Hannah Turner
Nicola Parker

First published in the United Kingdom 2008 by
Interpet Publishing
Vincent Lane
Dorking
Surrey
RH4 3YX

ISBN: 978 1 84286 182 0

Printed and bound in China.

This book has been published with the intent to provide accurate and authoritative information in regard to the subject matter
within. While every reasonable precaution has been taken in preparation of this book, the author and publisher expressly disclaim
responsibility for any errors, omissions, or adverse effects arising from the use or application of the information contained herein.
The techniques and suggestions are used at the reader's discretion and are not to be considered a substitute for veterinary care. If
you suspect a medical problem consult your veterinarian.

INTERPET
P U B L I S H I N G

www.interpet.co.uk

Chinchillas

DAVID ALDERTON

Table of Contents

Chapter 1

Why I Adore My
Chinchilla

Chinchillas, or "chins" as they are affectionately known, are growing rapidly in popularity as pets today, thanks to their cuddly appearance and friendly nature. They are not difficult to care for and can soon become very tame, particularly if you start out with a young chinchilla. Their care is quite straightforward, and provided that they are housed in suitable surroundings and their specific dietary needs are met, you are unlikely to face costly vet bills. One of the great advantages of chinchillas, compared to other pet rodents such as hamsters, is their much longer life span. It is not uncommon for chinchillas to live for 15 years or more.

Natural History

Understanding the physiology and behaviour of wild chinchillas can be helpful when interacting with your pet because domestic chinchillas still retain many of their instinctual traits and physical attributes.

Chinchillas belong to a group of rodents known as the caviomorphs. They are therefore related to guinea pigs and share a number of their characteristics. One of the most significant things that sets caviomorphs apart from the largest group of rodents called the myomorphs (which includes rats and mice) is a difference in their breeding habits. Caviomorphs have small litters born after a long gestation period, which lasts about four months in chinchillas. The young look just like smaller versions of their parents at birth. They have their eyes open and are able to move around immediately. By comparison, myomorphs breed much more rapidly, and their offspring are naked and helpless at birth. Caviomorphs also tend to attain a larger size, with the world's largest living rodent, the capybara (*Hydrochaeris hydrochaeris*), being a member of this group.

In the Wild

The natural habitat of the chinchilla is high in the Andes Mountains of South America. The thick, plush fur they are known for protects them and helps them survive the bitter cold in the Andes. Their distribution range consists mainly of Peru, Bolivia, Chile, and Argentina.

These rodents live in mountainous areas at altitudes up to 16,500 feet (5000 m), where the temperature may

Best known for their luxuriant, plush fur, chinchillas are native to the Andes Mountains of South America.

Chinchilla Taxonomy

All domesticated chinchillas today are believed to be descended from the long-tailed chinchilla (*Chinchilla lanigera*). Although they were once regarded as a single species in the days they were first discovered, zoologists have since recognised the short-tailed chinchilla (*Chinchilla brevicaudata*) as a separate species in its own right.

become very hot during the day and fall back significantly at night. In some areas, chinchillas occupy rocky retreats, but often they live in underground burrows that they dig themselves. Their distribution appears closely allied to that of a large terrestrial bromeliad plant, locally known as cardon (*Puya berteroniana*). Sometimes, chinchillas also share their accommodation with other creatures as well, notably chinchilla rats (*Abrocoma* species), which bear a distinct similarity to them, despite having an obvious rat-like tail. They do not interbreed, however.

Chinchilla colonies formerly numbered in the thousands in suitable areas. Today, however, the largest known group consists of no more than 500 individuals, with most groups comprising fewer than 50 individuals.

There can be difficulties, though, in terms of finding and counting chinchillas because they are shy by nature, and their lifestyle helps them avoid detection. Their large eyes reveal that they are crepuscular by nature, which means that they will only emerge from their hiding places in search of food when darkness starts to fall.

Physical Characteristics

Wild chinchillas are a greyish shade, which helps them blend in with the background of their environment, although even this may not be sufficient to protect them from all predators. Owls, in particular, possess excellent nighttime vision and represent a serious threat because they are able to fly silently and swoop down without warning. The chinchilla's large ears may sometimes help to detect the approaching danger, however, because his hearing is quite sensitive.

Living in colonies also brings some survival advantages, making it easier for these rodents to detect the presence of foxes that prey on them, thanks to the presence of many eyes and ears in the group. Chinchillas are reluctant to stray far from their burrows so that they can scurry back quickly to relative safety if danger threatens.

Their large whiskers also help chinchillas orientate themselves in darkness. These are thickened, specialised hairs that have a sensory function that allows them to determine whether they can squeeze safely into a gap.

Chinchillas are crepuscular animals, which means they are mostly active at night.

The other obvious feature of a chinchilla's body is the discrepancy in the size of his limbs. His front legs are much smaller than his hind legs. Chinchillas rely largely on their powerful hindquarters when moving. The lower part of their hind legs is relatively free from fur, especially on the underside, with the area further up the leg being well muscled to allow them to run quickly if required. Because they are exceptionally agile creatures, they are also able to hop and jump well. Chinchillas can even clamber over rocks and other obstacles using their short front legs. This is of real benefit in an environment where the ground may slope steeply because it helps them move quickly while maintaining balance. It can make the difference between life and death for an individual seeking the safety of his burrow when being pursued by a fox.

Because they are able to support their weight on their hindquarters, chinchillas can have a relatively good view of their environment. With various members of a group remaining alert in this way, ambushing them becomes a much harder task. The furred tail of chinchillas also helps them maintain their balance when sitting or standing on their hind legs. The fur here is longer and has a coarser texture than on the body itself.

The digits on the chinchilla's front paws are rather specialised, and they are often used like fingers. This allows a chinchilla to pick up and nibble pieces of food, as well as groom himself regularly, which is an important activity.

Chinchillas Today

In the past, chinchillas were all considered to belong to a single species, but today, zoologists divide them into two separate species, although both are found throughout their range. Those who are kept as pets are thought to be descended from the long-tailed chinchilla (*Chinchilla lanigera*), which is now found only on Cordillera de la Costa and the Andean slopes of Chile. A special protected area known as the Las Chinchillas National Reserve has been established in this region in an attempt to increase their numbers. In the past, early European travellers documented seeing thousands of these rodents there, but now their total population is thought to consist of no more than 5,500 individuals.

The short-tailed chinchilla (*Chinchilla brevicaudata*) is considered to be even more endangered, and the situation is worsening. Despite being protected, the species is now believed to have died out in Lauca National Park, a global biosphere reserve established in northern Chile in 1970. To the east in Bolivia, it has also become scarce, although it used to have a wider distribution than its long-tailed cousin. The subspecies called the king chinchilla (*Chinchilla brevicaudata chinchilla*) is already extinct in the wild. A single preserved example of

this race is on display at Frankfurt's Senchenberg Museum in Germany, serving as a sad testament to the mass slaughter of a unique and rare species.

Back in the 1970s, it was even thought that long-tailed chinchillas had died out, but during the middle of that decade, they were rediscovered in Chile. Although they are now strictly protected and there is no trade in their fur, the future for the remaining populations appears uncertain. Today, habitat changes are a major threat to their continued long-term survival in the wild. As a result, the surviving colonies are increasingly at risk of becoming isolated in small enclaves because they are unable to move into other areas and form new colonies with neighbouring chinchillas. This then makes it difficult for any increase in numbers to take place. An additional problem is that chinchillas do not have a high reproductive rate, so any increase in their numbers is naturally rather slow.

Nevertheless, there are groups working to promote the conservation of chinchillas in the wild by seeking

Life Span

Chinchillas potentially live for up to 20 years, which means that their development is slower than that of most pet rodents, whose life expectancies may be as short as two years. This in turn means that chinchillas are unlikely to be mature until they are at least seven months of age. Their gestation period is also lengthy as far as rodents are concerned, lasting around 111 days on average.

Because of the exportation of wild chinchillas for their fur in the early 1900s, they are now nearly extinct in their natural habitat and considered an endangered species.

and used the plush pelts to create magnificent gowns for their rulers. Chinchillas also were regarded as a source of food during that period.

When the Spanish invaded the region in the 1500s, they encountered these luxurious garments, which led to a limited export of chinchilla fur to Europe, where it was highly prized and often incorporated into the clothing worn by royalty. It was not until the 1800s that a massive surge in demand for the fur occurred, resulting in chinchillas being hunted in ever-increasing numbers. Records reveal that between 1840 and 1916, at least 7 million pelts were exported from Chile alone, and estimates suggest

to protect their habitats. They are also working through education by encouraging local children to be more aware of these small animals while involving landowners in conservation projects as well. The overall aim is to ensure that people and chinchillas can coexist in harmony.

Early Human Contact With Chinchillas

The chinchillas' earliest contact with humans occurred during pre-Columbian times. They came to the attention of the Incas, who desired them for their thick, silky coats

Why Chinchilla?

The descriptive name of the chinchilla was given to these unique little rodents by the Spanish, who encountered them following their invasion of South America during the 1500s. Their name commemorates that of the Chincha Indian tribe. Chinchillas were hunted for food but were desired more for their pelts, from which the Chinchas made luxurious garments. The word "chinchilla" literally means "little chincha."

that the total number of chinchillas killed through their range could have been as high as 21 million individuals.

Trade at this level was clearly never sustainable. Before long, the numbers of these rodents plummeted, and by the 1920s, chinchillas were facing extinction. Up to this point, several attempts had been made to farm chinchillas, but they all failed. Then a mining engineer called Mathias F. Chapman, who had been working in the region for the Anaconda Copper Company, decided to see if he could succeed in breeding what were by then very rare animals.

The first problem he faced was obtaining breeding stock. In spite of his endeavours, he only succeeded in acquiring 11 suitable breeding chinchillas over a period of four years leading up to 1923. But Chapman eventually identified the problems that had beset earlier breeding attempts and transported his precious new breeding stock back to California, where they started to breed successfully and gradually increased in number. Once widely bred, their fur was used in the manufacture of garments worn by the wealthy, with 150 pelts required to create a single full-length coat. It was not until the 1960s, however, that they first started to attract the attention of the pet trade.

People eventually realised that

Chinchillas are very attractive, with their large ears, bushy tails, and silky fur—quite unlike the popular image of rodents.

11

Why I Adore My Chinchilla

chinchillas have much to offer as companion animals. They look very attractive, with their large ears, bushy tails, and silky fur—quite unlike the popular image of rodents. They are fastidious in their grooming habits, and their dense coat protects them from parasites. The thickness of the chinchilla's fur can be gauged from the fact that there can be as many as 80 different hairs growing from a single hair follicle, whereas humans only have one hair per follicle. Their popularity has since soared, and nowadays they are kept as pets in many different countries around the world.

Domestication

Chinchillas still rank as one of the more costly pet rodents, and this is essentially because of their slower reproductive rate. As domestication has proceeded, a number of different colour variants have emerged, and this has provided an additional focus of interest for breeders. Shows are also held in some areas, with the exhibition side of the chinchilla-keeping hobby likely to grow even more as new colours become more widely available.

Judging of the exhibits in a show does not entail comparing animals with each other but actually assessing them against the so-called "ideal" example of the variety concerned as described by the breed standard. This standard details all the desirable features that judges should be looking for in terms of the chinchilla's physical appearance, or "type" as it is often known, as well as his colouration. Some chinchilla

FAMILY-FRIENDLY TIP

Chinchillas as Children's Pets

Chinchillas are suitable as pets for older children, typically those who are at least seven years old, because they will be able to take some responsibility for the daily care of their pet. You will have to teach your child not to allow the chinchilla out of his quarters without your knowledge, however, and certainly not to take him outdoors, where he could easily run away and might tragically end up caught by a predatory animal.

organisations are now holding their own shows wherever support is strong enough, rather than simply having classes exhibited as part of other small animal events. If this aspect of keeping chinchillas appeals to you, search online to track down details of shows being held near you.

Chinchillas as Pets

Chinchillas are easy pets to care for, particularly because they can be accommodated without difficulty in the home or even in a flat. They require very little space, are reasonably inexpensive to keep, and are quiet by nature. Their feeding needs are easily met, in spite of the fact that these rodents do have very specific dietary requirements. Nevertheless, they need little more than special food pellets, which are widely available at most pet shops, along with good quality hay, although they can be given some fresh foods in small amounts as well.

If you decide to keep more than one chinchilla, you will find that they get along well together. Most can be tamed without difficulty. Unlike many rodents, they also do not have any unpleasant odour associated with them. They are very clean creatures, not suffering from fleas or similar parasites, and they keep their wonderful coats in top condition with regular dust baths.

The potential life span of these rodents means that you could end up with a pet that lives longer than either a cat or a dog. However, this is a responsibility that needs to be thought through carefully beforehand, especially if you are seeking to obtain a pet for a child because you could ultimately be left caring for the pet. Holiday times are rarely a problem, though, as it is usually very easy to find a friend or neighbour who can accommodate your chinchilla in your absence.

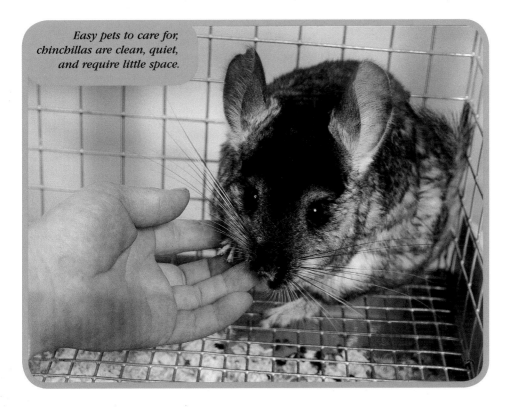

Easy pets to care for, chinchillas are clean, quiet, and require little space.

Choosing a Chinchilla

Chinchillas are becoming increasingly available through pet shops, although if you are looking for an unusual colour, you may have to find a breeder through a hobbyist magazine or the Internet. Ideally, start with a young chinchilla who is at least 16 weeks old and therefore fully weaned. He should come from an environment where he has become used to being handled, and so should already be quite friendly by this stage. Young chinchillas can be recognised by their smaller size compared to adults, but if you want to take on an older individual, there is no absolute guarantee of his age. It is almost impossible to determine how old a

chinchilla is once he is fully grown.

Do not rush the decision when it comes to choosing a chinchilla. After all, you are deciding on a companion who may be part of your daily life for as long as two decades, and this is a big commitment.

General Appearance

The first thing to ensure is that your potential pet is healthy, so start by looking closely at the chinchilla in his environment before attempting to pick him up. The droppings in his quarters should appear firm and dry, never loose, which is a sign of diarrhoea. This is a particularly serious condition in chinchillas. And although it may seem

A healthy chinchilla is bright-eyed, alert, and active, and his fur should be plush and soft in texture.

hardhearted, do not acquire one who is obviously ill because he may be difficult to nurse back to health.

Look also at the chinchilla's temperament. He should be bright-eyed, alert, and active. Although most chinchillas are sleepy during the day, they will soon wake up when being handled. Youngsters are especially lively by nature, and this is a good sign; adults are slightly less active.

The condition of the fur is important. It should be plush, standing out from the body, and soft in texture. If it appears flattened and matted, this is a sign of general ill health. The eyes should be bright and the ears should be free from any tears, which are reflective of past injury. There should be no discharge from the nose or signs of sneezing.

Before you pick up a chinchilla who appeals to you, ask the owner's permission. Handling him will give you an indication of his weight and also enable you to carry out a closer check on his health. With rodents, it is especially important to examine the incisor teeth at the front of the mouth. You can do this by gently pulling down the fur on the chin so that you can see the lower incisors. Place your fingers on each side of the upper jaw as well to lift the skin and check that both pairs of incisors are present and meet normally. On occasion, a tooth may be broken or deviated in some way, which will make it difficult for the chinchilla to eat normally. This may be reflected by a loss of weight and body condition.

Dental problems are not just

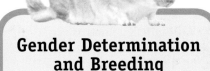

Gender Determination and Breeding

Gender is particularly significant if you are seeking to house chinchillas together, whether you intend to breed them or not. To identify whether a chinchilla is male or female, pick the individual up and turn him or her belly up. The spacing between the two orifices close to the base of the tail provides the best means of determining gender. The ano-genital gap is relatively short in the case of females but is much longer in males. Once a male chinchilla is about three months old, the testes will become apparent as swellings in this intervening space. In the case of adult chinchillas, it actually can be possible to distinguish the sexes without having to pick them up. Mature male chinchillas are generally not as large overall as females, and their heads appear proportionately bigger.

encountered in older chinchillas; they can afflict younger individuals too. The failure of the teeth to meet correctly, known as dental malocclusion, is often

The standard chinchilla colour is grey, although an increasing number of colourations and varieties are now available through selective breeding.

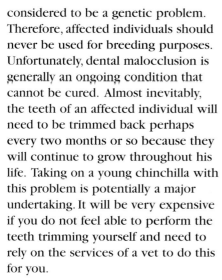

considered to be a genetic problem. Therefore, affected individuals should never be used for breeding purposes. Unfortunately, dental malocclusion is generally an ongoing condition that cannot be cured. Almost inevitably, the teeth of an affected individual will need to be trimmed back perhaps every two months or so because they will continue to grow throughout his life. Taking on a young chinchilla with this problem is potentially a major undertaking. It will be very expensive if you do not feel able to perform the teeth trimming yourself and need to rely on the services of a vet to do this for you.

Colours

An ever-increasing range of chinchilla colour varieties is now available, with the normal form traditionally described as the standard. There are some variations in colouration, however, in which certain individuals appear much darker than others. Their fur is bluish–grey and is darkest on the upper area of the body, with the under parts paler in colour. Close examination of the fur shows that the individual hairs in the coat are banded down their length. This alternating pattern of three dark bands with intervening paler areas is known as agouti and often can be seen quite clearly when you part the fur. There is also a mutation in captive stock in which the agouti banding is missing and the dark colouration running down the hairs is solid; these chinchillas tend to appear darker as a result. The chinchillas' colouration camouflages them in the Andean region where they dwell, helping them blend with the vast rocky, mountainous areas.

Pale Colourations

The first colour variants of the chinchilla were recorded in the 1950s, and prominent among these were white varieties that are still popular today. The Wilson's white, named after the original breeder, can be distinguished from other whites because it is not a true albino form. It has dark rather than pink ears and black instead of reddish eyes, although like a true albino, the fur is pure white. There is also a pink–white variety that more closely resembles the albino, although it still retains some pigmentation on the body, having faint beige tipping known as veiling on the fur.

There is also now a pied form called the mosaic that has highly variable markings. Some mosaics are predominantly white in colour with relatively small darker areas of fur, whereas other individuals, perhaps born in the same litter, may display much more extensive dark markings. It is impossible to predict the likely patterning of the offspring from that of the parent in the case of the mosaic variety.

Attractive beige-coloured forms are now quite common;

they are a champagne shade with white under parts. These are frequently described on the basis of the name of the breeder who was responsible for developing a particular strain, such as the Willman beige. They can vary in depth of beige colouration, with lighter-coated individuals having an almost creamy appearance. These individuals are sometimes rather confusingly also described as pearls, whereas those with darker-beige colouration are referred to as pastels.

Darker Colourations

A number of the varieties that have arisen in chinchillas are darker than the standard in colour. The first example of this type was the black velvet, which was developed in 1956. It has since become popular, thanks to its sleek appearance. These chinchillas are pure black in colour with a contrasting

Although a single chinchilla will do well with adequate love and attention, most seem to be happier kept in pairs.

white belly. There is also now a paler charcoal variant. Its colouration is greyer than that of the black velvet; it is a less dense shade of black that is sometimes also described as the ebony.

There is also both a brown velvet, where the colouration of the upper parts of the body is solid corresponding to that of the black counterpart, and an ordinary brown variant, which displays less intense brown colouration equivalent to the charcoal.

One of the most unusual and more recent chinchilla mutations is the violet, which was developed in Zimbabwe. It is a pointed variety, which means that it has darker colouration evident on the extremities of the body and on the face, feet, and tail, somewhat similar to a Siamese cat in terms of its patterning. Other rare colour variants are encountered occasionally, such as the sapphire, which is gunmetal blue with

white under parts. Others will almost certainly emerge in the future.

The increasing range of new colours is significant as far as chinchilla exhibitors are concerned, offering them greater scope for competition. Each variety may ultimately end up with an individual standard for judging purposes and may be grouped in separate classes as well. As far as pet owners are concerned, though, this is not especially significant simply because the temperament of the different mutations does not vary to any noticeable extent. You are likely to find that the rarer colours are

You can obtain a chinchilla from a breeder or pet shop, or you can adopt one from a local shelter or rescue.

more expensive to purchase than the standard colour.

Male or Female?

There is not really much difference between a male and a female chinchilla as a pet because both are likely to prove equally friendly. Do not be tempted to acquire a pair of chinchillas at the outset unless you are certain that you have the time and inclination to care for them and their offspring. If you think that you want to follow this path in the future, however, you can do so easily if you start out with just a single female. Never purchase a male and female chinchilla from the same litter for breeding purposes because they will be closely related, and this may increase the risk of birth deformities and a decline in litter size.

Consider Adoption

A number of chinchillas end up homeless for various reasons, and you may want to approach an animal rescue charity in your area to see if it has a suitable chinchilla who needs rehoming. Bear in mind these pets may have been neglected or mistreated. As a result, they are unlikely to be as friendly as a young chinchilla who grows up in your home; with patience, though, you may be able to win their confidence. Always be prepared to give a donation when acquiring a chinchilla under these circumstances so that the rehoming programme can continue for those chinchillas still in need.

Chapter 2

The Stuff of
Everyday Life

You'll need to organise everything you require for your chinchilla's care before bringing him home. You must decide what sort of housing setup you want, as well as buy food, feeding bowls and a water bottle, and a supply of bedding material and furnishings. Not everything your pet should have in his enclosure may be available from your local pet shop either. You will probably have to purchase wood to make a shelf and possibly build a nest box, too, if you are not buying one.

Chinchillas require relatively spacious housing, not just because of their size—they are one of the largest pet rodents—but also because they are lively by nature. You therefore need to think carefully about where your pet can be accommodated in your home at the outset. Choose an area where you can see your chinchilla easily and where you can enjoy watching him play. The location should also give you the opportunity to interact with him daily, which will then help as far as the taming process is concerned.

Where to Keep Chinchillas

Like other rodents, chinchillas are rather nervous by nature, simply because they feel instinctually vulnerable to predators. Even though they have been bred for many generations in captivity, they have not lost this fear. As a result, they are likely to feel stressed if exposed in the centre of a room because their housing can be approached from all sides. It will be much better, therefore, if you can position your pet's quarters against a wall, preferably in the corner of a room, depending on the position of nearby furniture. If your chin can only be approached from the front and possibly one side of his enclosure, he will feel more relaxed.

Likewise, your chinchilla's quarters need to be relatively tall to allow him to jump and clamber as chins do in the wild, so do not rest your pet's cage on the floor. Towering over him like a potential predator will probably cause him distress, which will make him

Chinchillas and Heat

Chinchillas are essentially indoor pets and cannot be kept outdoors for climatic reasons. They are susceptible to heatstroke and are also vulnerable to illness in damp surroundings. Once the temperature rises above 75°F (24°C), you will see them start to show signs of heat stress. As a way of trying to lose heat from their bodies, they stretch out rather than remaining hunched or curled up as they normally do. Their respiratory rate changes, with their breathing becoming more laboured.

You must take action at this stage, transferring your chinchilla to a cooler environment where he will not be exposed to drafts. Placing a fan that is blowing out colder air in his vicinity will also help, but again, you need to be sure that he is not being exposed to a draft. Obviously, if your home has an air conditioning unit, your chinchilla should be kept in a room where you can set the temperature lower and more within his comfort zone.

Choosing a proper enclosure and cage furnishings is essential to the well-being of your pet.

more likely to scurry for cover when anyone is in the vicinity. A situation where you are at a similar height and can easily reach into his quarters from the side with your hand will be far less threatening to him.

You may have a suitable piece of furniture that will support the cage, or alternatively, you might consider seeking a cage that is supplied with a stand of some kind, although the unit must be secure. Raising the cage off the ground gives additional protection against drafts, and it should also keep your pet from being confronted by the family dog or cat. If you have a cat,

ensure that the cage is tall enough or positioned in such a way that it reaches close to the ceiling. This will prevent your feline from climbing up on top of the chinchilla's housing and menacing him from above.

Avoid placing your pet's housing in rooms that tend to overheat or in front of a window because when the heat of the sun is magnified by the glass, it is likely to cause him to suffer from heatstroke, a potentially fatal condition. In general, chinchillas do not like heat, so avoid a location next to a radiator as well. You may even need to be prepared to move your pet to a cooler spot in the summer if the weather becomes very hot.

A hall or stairway area of any kind is not an ideal environment to keep your chinchilla either because he is likely to be exposed to drafts. For similar reasons, he shouldn't be kept in the kitchen because he could be affected by toxic fumes, as well as sprays used to clean appliances. Kitchens also may become too humid or hot for your pet when you are cooking.

Although a child may want to keep her pet in the bedroom, this is not a good idea. As the occupant of the room is supposedly going to sleep, the chinchilla is just waking up, and his activity can easily provide sufficient distraction to keep a child awake. Being housed in this part of the home also means that there is less opportunity for the family as a whole to interact with the chinchilla and enjoy his company. The more interaction he has with family members, the happier he will be. Chins are social animals who need a daily dose of attention and affection, especially if you are only keeping one.

Housing

Various chinchilla cage designs are now on the market. They are frequently sold

The Expert Knows

Activity Cycle

Chinchillas are nocturnal, which means that they are most active from dusk onward. This makes them ideal pets if you are away at work or school during the day because they will be waking up when you come home. They will remain active overnight, particularly if their home is equipped with a play wheel—but you will need to ensure that it runs smoothly so as not to cause a disturbance that may keep members of the household awake. Be wary if you find that your chinchilla appears lethargic and is out during the day because this can be a possible indicator of ill health, especially if linked with other signs such as a change in the appearance of his droppings.

in flat packs, with the unit easily able to be assembled using special clips that attach to a set of mesh panels. A floor tray is normally included as part of the pack. Always choose the largest cage that you can accommodate to ensure that your chin has plenty of space to move around. He needs to be able to climb in his quarters, so the height is important. At an absolute minimum, the size of the quarters needs to be at least 2 feet x 2 feet (0.6 m x 0.6 m).

Flat-pack housing of this type made especially for chinchillas is preferable to using an indoor aviary because it tends to be more robust.

Lively by nature, chinchillas require relatively spacious housing so that they can move about and climb easily.

Custom-Made Cages

If you have difficulty purchasing the size of cage that you want, it may be possible to have the panels made up for you. Consider approaching businesses that fabricate aviaries and dog runs.

The mesh size of the wire should not exceed 1/2 inch (1.3 cm) square so as to minimise the risk of any injuries to your pet's feet, and it needs to be at least 16 G (16 gauge) in thickness. The door unit should be hinged so that it opens outward, which makes it easier to service the interior of the quarters.

The strong incisor teeth at the front of a chinchilla's mouth enable him to destroy plastic easily, including the protective covering on most cage bars. These materials also may upset his sensitive digestive system if swallowed, sometimes with potentially fatal consequences.

Another consideration to bear in mind is the size of the door opening. It must be sufficiently large to allow you to reach into the interior easily and lift your chinchilla out. Not all aviaries have large doors that are suitable for this purpose. If there is a plastic base, it needs to be attached in such way that it will be out of the reach of your chinchilla's teeth.

A solid floor inside the housing is recommended. Although a mesh floor

Retreats such as nest boxes help your chinchilla feel more secure in his quarters.

quarters is a shelf that allows him to rest off the ground. This will need to be combined with a nest box nearby where he can sleep during the day.

The typical dimensions for a nest box can be up to 20 inches (50 cm) long, with the height and width of the box about 10 inches (25 cm). The size of the entrance hole is very important because it needs to allow your pet easy access to the interior. On the other hand, it should not admit so much light that it deters him from sleeping. Taking these factors into account, an entrance hole of about 6 inches (15 cm) in

allows dirt to drop through out of reach of your chinchilla, it can place him at risk of injury. The spacing of the mesh strands is significant, with young chinchillas particularly at risk because their smaller feet could slip down through the mesh. Sitting on a mesh floor also can cause hair loss on the body and sores to develop on the feet. This usually won't happen with a solid base, but you will have to spend more time cleaning the quarters and removing droppings so that there is no risk of illness and to keep your chin's luxuriant coat from becoming soiled.

The Importance of Retreats

Another basic design element that should be included in your chinchilla's

Bedding Warning!

Avoid sawdust as bedding material because of its fine nature—it is much dustier than shavings and is likely to cause repeated sneezing. It also can lead to eye irritation, especially because a chinchilla's eyes are so prominent. Old newspapers should not be used as bedding for chinchillas because they are likely to be shredded, possibly staining the fur, and because they may contain poisonous chemicals that could be harmful if consumed.

Your chinchilla's accommodations should include a food bowl and a dust bath, plus climbing facilities and toys.

diameter should prove adequate.

Chinchillas are, of course, not arboreal by nature. A nest box simply corresponds to the tunnels in which these rodents live in the wild. It will provide your pet with a snug retreat—not effectively off the ground, but simply one that is theoretically located further up the mountainside.

Some chinchillas also will take advantage of a retreat provided on the floor of their quarters. It should be in the form of a clay pipe, with a diameter at least as large as that of a nest box to provide easy access but still feel secure. It should also be relatively heavy and as such is better kept on the ground. Do not be tempted to substitute a lightweight plastic length of drainpipe because again, it is likely to be damaged by your chinchilla's teeth.

By offering a choice of retreats, you can help your pet feel more secure in his quarters. Perhaps rather surprisingly, chinchillas are more likely to show themselves if they have a range of places to hide from view within easy reach because this helps them feel safer and mimics their lifestyle in the wild.

Floor Coverings
Coarse wood shavings are most commonly used for bedding material, assuming that the cage has a solid base. It is vital only to buy shavings sold specifically for pet bedding. These should not be made from harmful types of wood and should be free from any toxic wood preservatives. Cedar wood, for example, contains potentially dangerous resins that will obviously be present in shavings of this type. Bedding doesn't have to be eaten to

cause ill effects; both dermatitis and respiratory problems may arise from exposure to unsuitable bedding.

Provide a relatively thick layer of shavings on the floor of your chin's quarters, at least 1 inch (2.5 cm) overall, so that he can maintain a good grip. A tool sold for spot cleaning cat litter trays will be useful to help you keep the base of the enclosure clean. By removing droppings and uneaten food daily, you won't have to change the entire floor covering as often.

Furnishings

Besides having adequate space for movement, another practical reason for having a large floor area in your chinchilla's quarters is the number of items that will need to be included in it. These include a food bowl and a dust bath, plus climbing facilities and toys.

Climbing Branches

Whatever type of housing you choose, it will be necessary to include some branches. These will enable your chin to utilise the height of the cage in particular, helping him climb up and down from his resting shelf easily. The choice of branches is important. They should be cut from trees that are neither poisonous nor treated with chemical sprays of any kind in the recent past. This helps to protect chinchillas because in addition to running up and down these branches, they will also gnaw at the wood itself.

Certain fruit trees such as apple and sycamore are generally safe, but other trees such as cherry, yew, and laburnum are likely to be toxic. All branches should be relatively thick so that they will support a chinchilla's weight, and ideally quite straight, which should make it easier to fix them in place. They must be secure so that they cannot be dislodged and fall down within the cage, causing injury or even death as a consequence. Avoid trying to wire the branches in place, though, because this could end up trapping your pet's feet. It is better to attach

Preparing Cage Branches

Before placing branches in your pet's enclosure, scrub them in a bucket of hot water using a clean brush. This will remove any greenish algae growth or wild bird droppings that will contaminate the wood and be harmful if ingested. Ideally, choose wood that appears clean at the outset.

Do not be tempted to clutter the interior with a number of thin branches because one or two thicker pieces are sufficient. Thinner branches cut into short lengths also can be provided separately on the floor of the cage for your chinchilla to gnaw on.

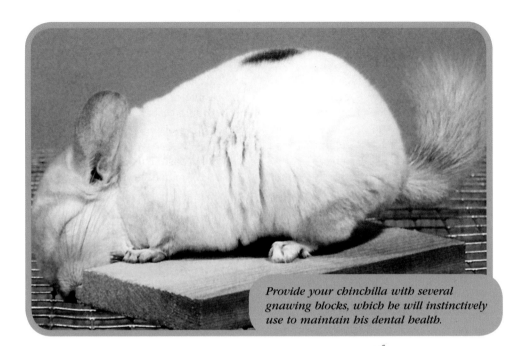

Provide your chinchilla with several gnawing blocks, which he will instinctively use to maintain his dental health.

them using a clamp or screw-type fixture, depending on how they are positioned. If a branch starts to become badly gnawed, be prepared to replace it before it collapses.

Food and Water Containers

Dry food should be kept separate from fresh food items that you offer your pet, but in both cases, a heavy earthenware bowl like the ones usually sold for use with dogs or cats is recommended. Plastic containers are easily destroyed by a chinchilla's teeth and are too light. Heavier bowls work best because they are more difficult to tip over. Also, food spills can potentially leave your pet without a reliable food source. Because they cannot be dislodged easily, stainless steel containers that hook onto the sides of the cage are another option. They cannot be damaged by a chinchilla's gnawing teeth, and again, are easily cleaned as necessary. Free-standing stainless steel bowls can, however, be tipped over by a chinchilla's weight, and so are far less suitable.

Never provide water in an open bowl. Aside from the risk of the bowl being tipped over and water soaking the bedding material, this type of container is easily polluted with cage debris and droppings. Bowls also use up valuable floor space—and worse yet, your chin's coat will become wet if he steps into the water. Instead, choose a water bottle that has a stainless steel spout with a ball in the tip that attaches to the outside of the cage.

This will enable your pet to drink without difficulty, provided that the spout of the water bottle is placed at a height roughly in line with (or just above) his mouth and not close to the ground.

A gravity-fed system is at work in the spout of water bottles of this type, so they shouldn't leak because water will only flow through it when the chinchilla is drinking and using his tongue to press back the ball. Occasionally, some chinchillas may manage to dislodge their water bottle or may even succeed in piercing the bottle with their teeth. There are shields available that will help to prevent this from happening. It is also a good idea to position the water bottle on the cage in such a way that if it is dislodged for any reason, it will only fall a short distance and so is less likely to shatter.

Hay Racks

Another important piece of equipment that should be incorporated into your chinchilla's quarters is a place to provide hay. Although some owners favour wire hay racks, they may sometimes be dangerous because of their open-weave design. It's also not a good idea to scatter hay on the floor where it can be mixed up with bedding. An alternative is to use a separate heavyweight bowl to provide hay. You can cut it up into smaller pieces with scissors and tease it out into individual strands so that it is less likely to be dragged around the cage. Additionally, this method gives you the opportunity to remove any unwanted plants such as thistles.

Exercise Wheels

Exercise wheels provide an excellent opportunity for chinchillas to cover relatively long distances by paddling around in them, which simulates activity they are naturally accustomed to in the wild.

A wheel must be totally enclosed, however, with no gaps between the rungs through which a chinchilla's foot might slip. Furthermore, it must fit snugly up against the side of your chinchilla's accommodation so that there will be no risk of injury, particularly to the tail, which might otherwise become trapped and is especially vulnerable to getting hurt or broken.

Homemade Toys

You can make a number of items for your chinchilla that will offer him entertaining places to hide away in or explore in his quarters. Wooden houses of any type are likely to be favoured, and they can be quite elaborate in design. However, do not paint or stain anything you make because these materials are likely to be toxic if gnawed in any way. You can give small wicker baskets of suitable dimensions to your chinchilla, although these too are likely to end up being destroyed by chewing.

Chews

The four sharp incisor teeth at the front of a chinchilla's mouth will continue growing throughout his lifetime. This is actually beneficial under normal circumstances because of the amount of wear to which these particular teeth are subjected. If they did not continue to grow, it would soon become impossible for a chinchilla to continue eating. What can happen, however, is that a chin may not use his teeth sufficiently in the confines of a cage. As a result, the incisors are likely to become overgrown, hampering the animal's ability to eat.

You should therefore provide your chinchilla with several gnawing blocks that he will instinctively use to maintain his dental health. Most pet shops offer a range of safe blocks, but only choose those that are made of wood rather than types such as those sold for dogs. Because these other types of pet chews may contain nutrients, they could upset your pet's digestive system.

Bathing and Grooming Equipment

You will need a bath for your chinchilla. Bathing is essential to maintaining the quality of his coat, although this bath will not contain water but a special dust.

Chinchilla baths are now commercially available. They are usually designed with a translucent plastic cover that sits over a tray, with a hole at the front through which a chinchilla can enter. The clear plastic allows you to watch your pet bathing while at the same time preventing the fine powder from scattering outside of the cage. This is important because some owners may be allergic to the dusting powder, which is similar to the volcanic ash that chinchillas use in the wild to keep their fur in top condition. Bathing in dust helps to remove greasy oils from the coat. Do not be tempted to use sand of any type because it could be carcinogenic.

Broad-sided trays have traditionally been used for chinchilla baths and are still available. These offer an advantage if you have more than one

31

Cage Cleaning Schedule

Daily: Provide fresh drinking water and food in clean containers.
As needed: Spot clean bedding on the floor. Replace branches that are chewed.
Weekly: Change the floor covering entirely and wash food bowls and water bottles.
Monthly: Strip down and clean the quarters thoroughly using a special pet disinfectant.

chin because they can share a bath. Chinchillas often seem to like the opportunity to bathe in this way. As well as having a practical purpose, bathing can be a social activity.

Where hand grooming is concerned, you will need to have a suitable comb. Regular combing will prevent your chinchilla's hair from becoming matted. A comb will be especially important during the moulting period when the coat is shed because it helps to strip out loose hairs.

Carriers

It is never safe to transport chinchillas in cardboard boxes because their sharp incisor teeth will allow a determined individual to escape easily from such confines. Therefore, it's always a good idea to invest in a secure pet carrier. Aside from using it to take your chin to the veterinarian or offering him a sheltered haven when you travel, a carrier will be useful on a regular basis because you can transfer him into it when you clean his quarters. Doing this is much safer than allowing him to wander about the room because your attention will be elsewhere, and you may not see your pet getting into a dangerous situation.

A small travelling crate like the ones sold primarily for small dogs or cats is appropriate. Many carriers of this type are designed in such a way that

FAMILY-FRIENDLY TIP

Children and Responsible Pet Care

Children love chinchillas, partly because of their cute appearance and their soft fur. But parents must be prepared to oversee most of the work involved in caring for any pet to ensure that all his needs are being met. It is particularly important to stress that children must never give their pet sweets or anything other than a few specific healthy treats without adult supervision; this could not only upset a sensitive digestive tract but might even prove to be fatal. You must also establish the rule that the pet is only to be handled when you are there, and show your children how to do so safely.

Social animals, chinchillas require more than routine care; they need a daily dose of attention and affection, especially if you are only keeping one.

they are collapsible and can be folded flat when not in use. If you use one of these, just make sure that it is securely fastened together when you reassemble it, and be sure to line it with some fresh shavings. You also need to ensure that the door of the carrier is always securely closed so that there is no possibility that a chinchilla could escape from the carrier in transit.

Cage Maintenance

Chinchillas are not messy pets, so it's relatively easy to keep their quarters clean. A dustpan and brush basically will be all that you require to sweep out the cage. You will also need a bucket and a scrubbing brush for washing it out. To remove soiled bedding, tip the cage litter straight into a refuse container, sweeping up any that spills. The water bottle can be cleaned in hot soapy water with a bottle brush, and the food bowls can be scrubbed easily in this way as well.

It helps if you can wash the various parts of the cage outdoors. Make up a disinfectant solution following the product directions closely. Clean off as much dirt as possible before washing everything because it may reduce the germ-killing strength of the disinfectant. When you are done, rinse the cage and equipment thoroughly with clean hot water. Shake the components to remove as much water as possible and wipe them dry with paper towels before reassembling the cage. Only replace the bedding after it has dried thoroughly because chinchillas should not be exposed to damp surroundings.

Preparing New Equipment

It is always a good idea to wash off all new equipment, just to ensure that it is thoroughly clean. Good hygiene is also particularly significant when you bring new pets home because they are most likely to fall ill following the stress of a move. Young individuals are especially vulnerable because the immune system that helps to protect against infection may not be as effective at this age as it is in adults.

By having everything ready and in place, you can simply transfer your new chinchilla to his home with minimal disturbance. If you have decided to keep more than one chinchilla, try to obtain both individuals at the same time so that they can be placed in their new quarters together. This

will be much easier than trying to introduce a second chinchilla at a later stage. If you are thinking of breeding chinchillas in the future, however, you will obviously need a different setup that will accommodate more than one individual.

Early Days

With everything prepared, you can place a new chinchilla in his quarters as soon as you get him home. Leave him there quietly to explore his new surroundings and settle down.

Keep a discrete watch to ensure that he has eaten and drunk by the next day. You can mark the water bottle with a felt-tip pen for this purpose. If you have young children, reinforce the door closure with a padlock so that you can avoid the risk of the door being opened in your absence, which could lead to your chinchilla escaping into the room and getting lost and frightened.

Do not be disappointed if your chinchilla appears nervous at first. This is quite normal, and it will take him time to settle into his home with you. By providing a number of hiding places, you have helped him feel more secure because he knows that he can dart back into them if he feels threatened, rather than being left in the open.

Allow your chin to stay essentially undisturbed over the first couple of days, although you will need to keep watch to ensure that he is eating properly and that his droppings are normal. It is particularly important not to change his diet at this stage because this can trigger a digestive disturbance. Continue to offer the food that he has been accustomed to, even if you decide that you want to change it at a later date.

Making Progress

Looking after a chinchilla's daily needs is quite straightforward. Hopefully, within just a few weeks of acquiring your pet, you will already be noticing just how much friendlier he has become as the result of the time you spend with him. By providing him with a proper home and spending quality time daily, you will continue to develop the bond between you.

Chapter **3**

Good Eating

Proper nutrition is an important aspect of any pet's daily needs, and it is essential to his good health. Although it is very easy to feed chinchillas, you need to have an understanding of how their digestive system works. Otherwise, they are likely to suffer from serious health problems. Because chinchillas don't adjust quickly to changes in their diet, they are also susceptible to digestive disturbances if fed unsuitable food.

Diet in the Wild

Chinchillas are vegetarians, although not a great deal is known about which plants are most important as far as their diet in the wild is concerned. Their digestive system is well adapted to breaking down this type of food and obtaining maximum nutritional benefit from it.

The incisor teeth at the front of a chinchilla's mouth have an important part to play in this process, allowing him to nibble cleanly through even tough plant stems without difficulty. This is because of the teeth's sharp cutting edge; they are not flat but slope and are shaped rather like a chisel. There is a thicker covering of hard enamel on the front of the incisor teeth, with an area of soft dentine behind that wears away more rapidly, maintaining this sloping profile.

There is also a long gap in the jaws extending back behind the cheek teeth. This is very significant for vegetarian rodents like chinchillas because it means that while the rodent is nibbling at shoots, he can effectively pull in the skin of his cheeks behind the incisors. This folded skin then acts rather like a curtain, ensuring that the animal cannot accidentally swallow any small stones or other debris while feeding, which might cause him to choke.

The vegetation on which chinchillas feed can be tough, especially because they live in relatively inhospitable surroundings where environmental conditions are naturally harsh. After nibbling the plant matter with their incisor teeth and tearing it into pieces that can be swallowed easily, they will

Chinchillas subsist on a vegetarian diet in the wild

Will Tunnel for Food

Suitable food is scarce in the Andean region of South America, which is the chinchilla's native home. These animals are forced to feed largely on dry grasses, as well as forage for the leaves and shoots of small, low-growing shrubs in the region. The arid nature of the landscape means that cacti are common here, and chinchillas have evolved ways to overcome the sharp spines that are associated with these plants to feed on them as well. The quisco cactus is a tall-growing species that may attain a height of up to 13 feet (5 m). It produces fruits called guillaves, of which chins are very fond. Often impatient for the fruit to fall to the ground, they have evolved an unusual way to reach it before it has fallen.

Obviously, chinchillas cannot clamber up the outside of a cactus because of the spines that would painfully stick into their bodies. Instead, they use their sharp teeth to tunnel into the firm core of the cactus, clambering up from the inside. Presumably, their sense of smell allows them to know when they have reached a level where there is fruit on the outside of the cactus. They then use their sharp incisors to gnaw their way through to the outside to reach the guillaves. These cacti are slow-growing, and so undoubtedly, successive generations of chinchillas have tunnelled in and out of them in this way, with minimal obvious impact on the plant itself because it has continued to flourish.

then chew it up using the molar teeth at the back of the mouth.

The Digestive Process

The natural food of chinchillas is low in nutrients, which means that relatively large quantities need to be consumed to meet their nutritional needs; this demands an efficient digestive system. Unfortunately, this biological process is not easy. Chinchillas are forced to rely on beneficial microbes (in the form of bacteria and unicellular organisms called protozoa) to break down the cellulose that is present in the cell walls of plant matter so that they can digest their food properly.

There is a blind-ending sac, known as the caecum, at the junction between the small and large intestines where these microbes are primarily located. The caecum corresponds to the human appendix. It is relatively large in chinchillas because it is here that the digestive process occurs. The bacteria and protozoa only operate effectively within a narrow set of environmental conditions; any changes in the relative acidity (pH) in this part of the gut means that not only will they cease

Feeding Schedule

Some chinchilla owners prefer to offer their pets a restricted amount of pellets each day, typically about 2 tablespoonfuls daily for an adult and slightly more for youngsters who need additional nutrients to support their growth. Pregnant and nursing females require additional food as well.

A number of keepers follow what is often described as an *ad-libitum* feeding method, which means providing chinchillas with access to an unregulated supply of food. This is safe because they generally do not overeat as far as their pellets are concerned, although it is a different matter if they are given unrestricted access to fresh foods. There are specially designed hoppers suitable for the free-feeding of pellets.

Daily: Measure out your chinchilla's food in the evening and provide it to him when he is waking up. Also, check whether more hay is required.

Later in the evening: Provide a treat, preferably at the same time each day, when you can be around to keep your chinchilla company so as to strengthen your bond with him.

Although it is very easy to feed chinchillas, you need to have an understanding of how their digestive system works.

to function effectively, but harmful bacteria also may start to flourish here instead, resulting in a severe digestive disturbance.

Diet Risks for Pet Chinchillas

In the wild, chinchillas have a fairly constant diet, which helps to keep the microbial population in their gut stable. Unfortunately, if you vary a pet chinchilla's diet significantly, it will alter the normal conditions within his intestinal tract and can kill off many of these necessary microbes. This means that he will not be able to digest his food properly and that he is likely to develop diarrhoea and suffer weight loss as a result. Changes to diet therefore need to be made over a period of several weeks, with daily adjustments being relatively slight so as to allow the microbial population to

adapt.

Fibre has an important role to play in the health of a chinchilla's gastrointestinal system. It helps to propel food through the digestive tract by bulking it out and ensuring that there is no major shift in the pH of the caecum, which is so critical to the chinchilla's overall well-being. Lack of fibre also can be linked with constipation because the food takes longer than normal to pass through the gut.

Basic Nutrients

The basic nutrients that chinchillas need are similar to those that humans require. They need protein for growth purposes, and they utilise carbohydrates primarily as a source of energy. Fat is used for insulation in the body and is incorporated into

Your chinchilla's nutritional needs are easily met with a quality pellet food, some fresh fruit and greens, hay, and clean water.

cell membranes. It also represents a concentrated energy store that can be broken down to meet the body's additional energy requirements if necessary.

Vitamins are required for a variety of purposes in the body. They can be subdivided into two groups: the fat-soluble vitamins such as vitamins A and D, which are stored in the liver, and the water-soluble vitamins such as the vitamin B complex, which is made up of a range of individual components such as thiamine (vitamin B1) or riboflavin (vitamin B2). Members of the vitamin B group are involved in metabolic processes that take place within individual cells. They are known as water soluble because they are not stored and can be washed out of the body via the kidneys. This potentially can result in a deficiency in some cases if these vitamins are not adequately provided or if they are absent from the diet altogether.

Chinchillas also require a range of inorganic chemicals in their diet known as minerals. Calcium and phosphorus, for example, are the key ingredients in making bone. Trace elements such as iodine, which are needed in lesser quantities, are also necessary to ensure that the body functions well.

Feeding Chinchillas

It may sound as if it is quite difficult to provide a suitable, balanced diet

Supplements

Various supplements, available both in powder and liquid form, can be used with chinchillas. While powdered supplements are usually sprinkled over the damp surfaces of fresh food such as a slice of apple, liquid supplements should be added to your chinchilla's drinking water. In most cases, though, unless your chinchilla is recovering from illness, there is no need to use supplementation of any kind because all your pet's nutritional needs should be met in his regular food pellets.

Additionally, there is a risk that if you use a supplement, your chinchilla could be at risk from a vitamin or mineral overdose. If you do resort to using one, do not exceed the recommended limits as a precaution. Rather than a general supplement, it may sometimes be necessary to offer a specific calcium supplement in the case of a pregnant female. This is something that your veterinarian can advise you about. For the safety of your pet, always check with the vet before using any kind of medication, vitamin, or product with which you have no previous experience.

for chinchillas, but in reality this is not the case. In the early days, when chinchillas were farmed for their fur, it soon became apparent that providing them with a standard supply of food was vital, both for the health of the animals themselves and also to make it easy to keep them on a large scale. Considerable research into their nutritional needs has since been carried out, and this has led to the development of pelleted diets that contain all the nutrients they need to remain in good health and to breed successfully.

Pellet Foods

Numerous pelleted diets are widely available at pet shops today. Chinchilla pellets themselves comprise a range of different ingredients not actually based on the type of food that these rodents would eat in the wild, but rather on items that are widely used in the animal foodstuffs industry. As a result, ingredients include items such as soybean and peanut meal, as well as alfalfa, which is a type of grass.

Various brands are sold, although the choice is far more limited than in the case of dry food marketed for dogs and cats, and distinctions among chinchilla diets are less significant as a result. Nevertheless, do not allow yourself to run out of food for your pet because you may find that the particular brand you use is out of stock at your local shop.

You can make changes to your chinchilla's dict, but the key to avoiding any risk to his health is to do so gradually rather than suddenly replacing one type of food with another. Again, because of this, it is a good idea always to keep a spare bag of food at home so that you will never run out.

Chinchilla food is marketed in packs of different sizes, but do not purchase a large quantity if you have a single individual. A chinchilla will only eat just over 1 ounce (30 g) of pellets per day as a general rule.

Always check the pack for its use-by date prior to purchase because the vitamin components will fall significantly in potency if you use out-of-date food, leaving your chinchilla's health at risk from nutritional deficiencies. You therefore need to be certain that you will be able to use up the pack contents before the use by date because otherwise you will have to discard it. On this basis, chinchillas are not expensive pets to feed.

The way in which food is stored is also important. Choose a relatively cool spot away from direct sunlight. Keep all packages sealed to exclude air, which can

The Expert Knows

Stick to Chinchilla Pellets

There are now many pelleted foods available for small pets, but it is not safe to use these for chinchillas. Rabbit pellets, for example, are likely to cause irreversible liver damage if fed to chinchillas. This is also a reason why chinchillas should not be housed with rabbits, even in a large enclosure, because they are likely to take the rabbits' food, not realising the harm it can cause them. In an emergency, guinea pig pellets are a safer option, but try to avoid using them. Even if the pellets themselves have no toxic side effects, the sudden switch in diet can have harmful effects.

Pellets that are specially formulated for chinchillas constitute the main part of their daily diet.

harm the vitamin content. You also must store food in a dry place. If the packaging becomes saturated and water reaches the contents inside, you will need to discard it simply because the dampness will trigger the development of harmful moulds that are likely to cause upset or illness in chinchillas eating the spoiled food.

The Importance of Hay

Another important ingredient that chinchillas require as part of their daily diet is hay. Hay is necessary because although pellets represent a concentrated source of nutrients, they do not contain sufficient amounts of the essential fibre that is needed as part of a balanced diet. The chinchilla's digestive system is adapted to eating relatively large volumes of vegetation that is low in nutrients in the wild, so commercial pellet formulas are often bulked up to account for this and to ensure that the animals stay healthy.

High-quality hay is essential. It can be purchased from most pet shops, ready packed in plastic bags. Hay made primarily of timothy grass is usually recommended, or alternatively, alfalfa hay can be used. Be very careful of other types of hay. You do not want to choose a variety that is dusty because it is likely to have harmful effects on your chinchilla's respiratory system, especially if the hay is stale or smells mouldy. Beware of other components in the hay that could be harmful, too, such as thistles or even

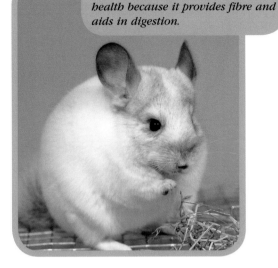

Hay is essential to your chinchilla's health because it provides fibre and aids in digestion.

sometimes poisonous plants.

Only purchase hay in relatively small quantities so that it will be as fresh as possible. Slice open the plastic bag to create a small hole through which you can extract hay as required. Store the bag in a dry location if possible. This should ensure that there is no risk of other rodents, such as mice, tunnelling into the supply. Should this happen, it will not be safe to use for chinchillas because of the possible risk of spreading disease from the mice.

The amount of hay that a chinchilla requires is about a handful daily, but it doesn't need to be measured out precisely. Although chins should always have a fresh supply available, you can just top it off as necessary. It is important to keep hay off the cage floor so that it does not become muddled up with bedding. You can use a special hay rack as mentioned

Finger Foods

Chinchillas use their front paws like hands to pick up their food, typically sitting up and supporting their weight on their hindquarters when feeding. This enables them to nibble off pieces of food that are too large to be swallowed whole.

previously, but it may be better to use one only with older animals because the lively nature and small size of young chins puts them more at risk of becoming trapped in them.

There is an alternative to using actual hay: alfalfa cubes, which are a form of hay. Not all chinchillas are willing to sample these, however, especially if they have always fed in the past on ordinary hay. The dense texture of the alfalfa cubes can be off-putting, so try breaking up one or two of the cubes slightly to see if this encourages a reluctant chinchilla to eat hay in this form. Until you are certain that your pet will eat these cubes, do not invest in a large quantity of them because you may not be able to persuade him to eat them regularly or at all.

Each chin will typically require about a cube every day. Do not leave your chinchilla without hay for any length of time because, again, this will upset his sensitive digestive system. It also may cause him to start pulling out his own fur to make up for the lack of fibre in his diet. Only restrict

the amount of hay you provide if you know that your pet has not eaten any for a while. Providing an unrestricted quantity may otherwise cause him to gorge himself under these circumstances. Therefore, simply measure out the usual daily amount for the first few days until his desire for hay is satiated.

Hay Mixes

Different types of hay can be mixed together, with each having slightly different nutritional properties. These can include oat, timothy, and alfalfa. Also, if you have a garden where Bermuda grass grows, it too can be added to the diet to offer some fibre variety. It is very important that the grass has not been treated with any chemicals, however, and as a further precaution, be sure to wash it off and shake it dry before offering it to your

For a balanced and varied diet, offer your pet small quantities of fresh vegetables.

Bad Eating

There are a number of unsuitable foods for chinchillas, particularly anything sugary. Sweets of all types are hazardous, particularly chocolate, which contains theobromine and has potentially deadly effects on the respiratory system. Any meat-based products also should never be offered to these rodents, along with fried foods of any kind. Most human foods, such as biscuits and cakes, are equally dangerous to a chinchilla's well-being. Never offer any salted or flavoured nuts of any kind, and only offer half a hazelnut or part of a peanut on occasion. Bear in mind that many plants and even avocado may prove toxic.

chinchilla. Never place it on top of the bedding before it dries completely because the dampness will cause shavings to stick to it, which would be harmful. It's better to provide it in a clean food container instead.

Vegetables

For a balanced and varied diet, offer your pet some fresh foods, but again, only in small amounts so as not to precipitate any digestive upset. When offering greens, avoid members of the cabbage family such as broccoli and brussel sprouts, which can give rise to gas production in the intestinal tract.

Vegetables that chinchillas can eat include red-leaved forms of lettuce, which are far more nutritious than ordinary green lettuce, and the tops of carrots. A piece of parsley or a small bit of chard are other possibilities. Beware of shop-bought vegetables, though, because they may have been sprayed with pesticides—only buy organic in this case.

The quantity of appropriate greens or vegetables that you offer should be restricted to prevent intestinal distress. It is not actually essential for chinchillas to be given greens. However, if you wish to provide them and your pet has not been used to eating them, increase the amount you are offering gradually. Large amounts are not required; one or two pieces each day will be adequate. Always wash and shake dry the stems, and if necessary, chop them up so that they will fit easily into a food dish. This will prevent your chinchilla from dragging his food across the floor of his quarters.

The other critical aspect when it comes to feeding greens or vegetables is that they must always be fresh. This ensures that your chinchilla receives maximum benefit from the vitamin content of the herbage and that he is not at risk from anything on it that can endanger his health. You can buy most

FAMILY-FRIENDLY TIP

Supervised Feeding

There are several things that a child can do to help to feed the family pet, such as measuring out the required daily quantity of pellets and pouring them into a clean food bowl. Under proper supervision, children also can pick greens for the pet as long as they have washed their hands first. In addition, they can take charge of growing and watering the plants that are intended as chinchilla food.

of what your pet requires in the way of fresh foods at a local supermarket or at your local farmers market.

Home Gardens

If you have a garden, you might enjoy growing a suitable range of fresh foods for your chinchilla, or you can do so in pots on a windowsill. This is a fun way to guarantee a constant fresh supply. You can either obtain packets of seeds for this purpose, which you can sow in suitable compost at home, or alternatively, you can purchase potted herbs from supermarkets or garden centres. Generally, those that have been cultivated for garden use rather than immediate culinary purposes tend to

be more robust for growing in this way.

Herbs for Chinchillas

Mint (*Mentha*) comes in many different varieties and is a hard, tough plant. If you are planting this in a garden, however, set some paving slabs in the ground so that you can curb its growth, because some strains can be very invasive, spreading via their vast root system underground. Keep it well watered in dry spells, and grow it in partial shade. In the winter, mint tends to die back, so if you want to continue having a fresh supply, you'll have to dig up some of the roots and transfer them to a flower pot, which you can grow in a well-lit part of the home until warmer weather returns.

There are also many different strains of basil (*Ocimum basilicum*) you can grow. This is a plant that requires relatively warm conditions and tends not to thrive outdoors in temperate areas, even in the summer.

Not all herbs suitable for chinchillas have an upright growth, as in the case of thyme (*Thymus*). This plant creeps over the ground, so if you want to grow it in a pot, it will trail down the sides. Thyme is a relatively hardy herb but needs to be cut back regularly to prevent the stems from becoming woody.

Oregano (*Origanum*) also has a relatively similar pattern of growth. It too can be cultivated easily in a corner of the garden, dying back during the winter in colder climates before sprouting up again in the spring. Cutting back the stems can encourage more growth, but it may be past its best offering by the summer.

There are some wild herbs that you can gather as well, with dandelion (*Taraxacum officinale*) leaves especially popular with chinchillas. Do not pick these from lawns or roadside verges, however, because they may have been treated with chemicals. Dandelion leaves tend to be most available in the spring and early summer, with a second flush of growth occurring during the early autumn in temperate areas. It is usually possible to find leaves throughout much of the year, though.

Dandelions are easy to cultivate during the winter period. Dig up several of the long whitish roots of these plants before the cold sets in, and chop them into lengths of about 1 to 2 inches (2.5 to 5 cm). Then set these pieces vertically into pots, with one end just protruding above the surface of the soil. This will ultimately be where the leaves develop. Keep the pots in a sunny warm spot. Within a few weeks, you should be rewarded with a crop of leaves that you can offer your chinchilla for a yummy snack.

Treats

Chinchillas, rather like humans, will not instinctively eat only what is good for them. This is why treats need to be strictly rationed. Although they provide a good way to tame your pet, too many goodies will have the same negative consequences that they do on the rest of us, namely ill health and obesity.

Visit any pet shop and you are likely to find an abundance of treats, some of which are intended specifically for chinchillas. The most important

Your chin will enjoy occasional treats, but be sure to offer healthy ones in small amounts.

How to Feed Treats

Rather than dropping treats in among your pet's regular food, put them in a separate small bowl instead. Otherwise, you are likely to find that the treats tend to be picked out and the regular food remains uneaten. Worse yet, your chinchilla may resort to emptying his entire food bowl all over the floor of his quarters in search of that tasty raisin.

Treats can be used to help to tame your chinchilla. Offer them by hand if they are large enough to pass to your pet easily, but bear in mind that your chinchilla may inflict a painful bite with his sharp incisors if your fingers are in the way, which may cause bleeding.

popular treats to offer is more likely to be found in grocery shops: raisins, which these rodents love. Dried fruits must be strictly rationed to a maximum of one per day, however, given on alternate days of the week. And no more than half a raisin twice a week should be fed to youngsters. This is because the chinchilla's digestive system is unable to cope with their high sugar content. Raisins, or other dry fruit such as cranberries, must be free from sulphites, so check the packaging. Also, they must never be covered in chocolate, which is likely to be deadly.

The black sunflower seeds that are widely sold as bird food are also very popular with chinchillas, but you should literally only provide them with the occasional seed to reduce any risk of these rodents becoming overweight, which will shorten their life span.

aspect when it comes to offering treats is to realise exactly what they are—something to be given in small quantities on an occasional basis rather than as a mainstay of the regular diet. If you are feeding prepared treats to your pet, follow the instructions for using them carefully.

As far as chinchillas are concerned, one of the most

To keep your pet healthy, keep an eye on his appetite and monitor his weight regularly.

These seeds have very high oil content.

On occasion, you may want to offer a little fresh fruit such as a small piece of sweet apple or grape as an alternative treat. Some vegetables, too, like a small piece of peeled carrot or celery also can be used as a special treat. But as a rule, never provide more than the equivalent of 1 teaspoon of such food daily.

Other Healthy Items

Chinchillas often like to gnaw on fresh twigs in their quarters. These boost the fibre content of their diet as well as help to keep their teeth trim. Twigs and branches should be cut from trees that are not harmful to your chin, either because they have been sprayed or because they are poisonous. Apple and elder are good choices.

Some owners provide other items for this purpose, including the volcanic rock known as pumice, which is something likely to be encountered in a chinchilla's natural environment. Aside from its dental benefits, pumice adds to their mineral intake as well.

Another item that is sometimes given to chinchillas is cuttlebone. It is not a true bone but rather a buoyancy aid present in the body of cuttlefish. By nibbling cuttlebone, chinchillas not only wear down their incisors, but they also may benefit from its high calcium content if they swallow fragments of it.

Water

Chinchillas need to have constant access to clean drinking water, particularly because a diet comprising pellets and hay provides relatively little fluid compared to what they might eat in the wild.

Ordinary domestic drinking water is normally satisfactory, but it may be beneficial to filter it so as to remove chlorine. Do not offer chilled water from a refrigerator as this may upset your chinchilla's digestive system. Bear in mind also that bottled water is not necessarily free from bacteria and therefore isn't any safer to use than tap water.

Chapter 4

Looking Good

Chinchillas are fastidious about keeping clean, even though their plush coats are so dense that they do not suffer from parasites such as fleas. Looking after their grooming needs is not especially difficult, but it is nevertheless an aspect of their care that is important to their overall well-being, apart from their appearance. Another benefit of caring for your chin's coat on a regular basis is that it can help to strengthen the bond between you and your pet.

General Grooming

It is important to get a chinchilla, especially a youngster, used to being groomed, simply because this task will need to be carried out probably about twice a week throughout his life. Grooming becomes particularly important when an individual is shedding his coat, which is a process that occurs about every three months.

Begin to accustom your chinchilla to grooming by keeping the first few sessions brief. Initially, if your chinchilla does not like being restrained, it may be better to try this during the middle of the day, when he is most likely to be sleepy. Also, try to avoid planning a grooming session if the weather is very warm because the stress of being caught and restrained may trigger the onset of heatstroke. In most cases,

you will have little option other than to catch your chinchilla because it will be nearly impossible to carry out this task if your pet remains in his quarters. Almost inevitably, he will not cooperate, seeking to hide away perhaps in his nest box, especially if he is sharing his quarters with a second chinchilla who is likely to be running around at the time. It may help if someone else restrains your chinchilla so that you can concentrate on grooming his fur. This will speed up the process and make it less stressful for all involved.

Special combs are available for grooming, and these can be purchased either from pet shops that stock chinchilla accessories or via specialist suppliers on the Internet. The only other thing you'll need is a secure table or countertop. Find a level surface at

Shedding Facts

You will be able to spot when your chinchilla is shedding because the coat will appear uneven, and there will be an obvious dividing line between the new fur and the remains of the old coat. Still referred to as the priming line, this term originated during the chinchilla's fur-farming past. The line effectively moves down the chinchilla's body from the head, with the moult completed once the tail is reached; this process is what causes the division in the fur to disappear. It was at this stage that the chinchilla's pelt was regarded as being in prime condition, which explains the origin of the term. Ranch (farmed) chinchillas were never handled, even to be groomed. This was because picking them up could have had an adverse affect on the quality of the pelt, and so they remained quite wild in contrast to their descendants now kept as pets.

a convenient height where you can groom your chinchilla easily without having to stoop down. Towering over your pet is likely to be frightening for him and may cause him to struggle more than he would otherwise.

The grooming process itself is quite straightforward. You simply need to comb your chinchilla's back initially, and then continue down the sides of the body to ensure that the fur there appears smooth. Do not forget to comb the longer fur on the tail and the sides of the face, taking care to avoid the eyes. Chinchillas are always combed and not brushed because of the texture of their coats.

Bathing

Chinchillas come from a part of the world where free-standing water is in short supply. Indeed, they may be compelled to eat vegetation covered with dew in their arid domains as a way of guarding against dehydration. Because they are unable to drink freely in the wild, they evolved a way of maintaining the condition of their fur without having to bathe in water that effectively takes the form of a dry shampoo.

You will need to purchase special chinchilla dust powder for this purpose, which is likely to be available from the same supplier as their food pellets. This powder is unique, being very fine in nature, and cannot be replaced by sand, which could even stain the coat in some cases. You will not need a large quantity of dust powder if you have just one or two

Regular grooming not only keeps your chinchilla looking good, but it improves his overall hygiene.

chinchillas, particularly because it is possible to reuse it more than once. Do not put previously used powder back into the bag with the new dust powder, however. For hygienic reasons, you should discard it after three or four uses. A layer of about 2 inches (5 cm) will be required in the bottom of the bath container to enable your chinchilla to bathe well.

Chinchilla Baths

Whatever type of container you supply as a bath, it must be large enough so

Grooming Supplies

You will need to obtain the following items to meet the grooming needs of your chinchilla:
- a dust bath
- chinchilla dusting powder
- a comb

that your chinchilla can roll around easily in the powder. This can be quite messy, and you may find that much of the powder is scattered in the surrounding area and sometimes in the bedding if there is not an adequate rim around the container. It is therefore a good idea to remove food bowls and any hay when you place the dust bath in your chinchilla's quarters to prevent them from becoming soiled by the loose powder.

The bath itself may take up a relatively large amount of floor space, depending on the dimensions of your pet's accommodation. Two chinchillas will require a correspondingly larger bath because both will almost inevitably

The Expert Knows

Self-Grooming

Chinchillas will groom themselves using their front paws to wipe their faces after eating certain foods such as sweet apple. You may find that certain foods such as carrot juice may stain the fur slightly on this part of the body, but these effects will only be temporary. You should not wash your chinchilla's coat, however. If it does become wet for any reason, allow it to dry off naturally; do not put your chinchilla in a warm place. He will find this uncomfortable and could even suffer from heatstroke as a result.

No Bathing Permitted!

Do not allow a pregnant chinchilla to dust bathe toward the end of her pregnancy because this may make her more vulnerable to an ascending infection of the reproductive tract.

want to bathe together, just as their wild relatives are inclined to bathe communally. Do not be surprised if young chinchillas are reluctant to dust bathe at first, especially if they do not have any adults who can show them the purpose of the bath. You may need to lift a youngster into his bath and rub some of the powder into the coat as a way of encouraging this behaviour.

Bathing Schedule

It is a good idea to provide a bath after you have combed your pet's coat. This is because combing will have opened up the fur, making it easier for the powder to penetrate down through the hairs. It serves to absorb the excess oils, stripping them out of the coat.

Once they appreciate the purpose of the bath, chinchillas will start rolling around within a few minutes of having the bath placed in their quarters, particularly at dusk, when they are likely to be awake. Allow them to bathe for about five minutes or so. They are likely to roll about both on their sides and back, with the dust penetrating the entire coat.

Chinchillas should be given bathing facilities on alternate days, although occasionally, particularly during spells of hot weather, they may require a more frequent opportunity to have a dust bath. It is possible to tell if dust bathing is required by the condition and the so-called "lie" of the coat. If the fur starts to become greasy, appears flatter than usual, and loses its soft texture, these indicators suggest that your chin requires a bath. Also, if the fur parts more than normal and does not hold together, a dust bath is necessary.

The readiness of chinchillas to bathe in this way means that you cannot allow them constant access to their dust baths. Excessive exposure to the powder can strip most of the natural oils from the coat, causing the skin to become excessively dry. If you notice that your chinchilla is scratching more frequently and intensely than normal, this is probably the reason. The problem should be resolved simply by reducing the frequency of the dust baths. Do not delay in taking this step or it will take longer for the condition of the skin to improve.

Dental Care

As with all rodents, the teeth of a chinchilla are vital to his well-being.

An adaptation to the arid climate in which they evolved, chinchillas maintain the condition of their fur and skin by taking dust baths.

Any distortion or damage to the teeth will have potentially harmful consequences, especially if the incisors at the front of the mouth are affected. This is because they act like scissors, chopping up food into pieces of suitable size for swallowing.

The most obvious sign of a dental problem is indicated by a change in a chinchilla's feeding habits. He will start to eat much more slowly than usual, sometimes with pieces of food dropping out of his mouth, depending on the cause of the problem. Chins can chip an incisor tooth easily in the confines of a cage, particularly if the individual is deficient in calcium. Other obvious issues could simply be the result of tooth decay.

The first line of defence is to catch your pet so that you can look at his incisor teeth and check if any have been damaged. Be aware that the source of the injury could also be farther back, affecting the molars. Check all teeth, and look at the condition of the mouth and gums as well.

A common difficulty occurs when an incisor tooth somehow becomes damaged and broken because its corresponding upper or lower tooth will continue growing unchecked. In normal circumstances, of course, both teeth wear down simultaneously by forming a discrete cutting surface. When seeking to correct a deformity of this type, you must prevent the undamaged tooth from growing in an uncontrolled manner by trimming it back as necessary. Hopefully, the other tooth will gradually regrow at the same time, although it too may need careful trimming to restore its cutting edge. Luckily, chinchillas' teeth grow rapidly, averaging around 3 inches (7.5 cm) over the course of a year, so that damage can soon be repaired.

Almost certainly, whether you can ascertain the source of a problem or not, you will need to seek the assistance of a veterinarian so that she can perform a dental checkup to find the specific source of the problem and provide treatment to correct it.

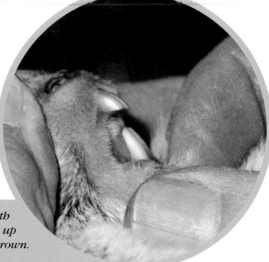

Check your pet's teeth frequently to make sure they line up correctly and are not overgrown.

Teeth Trimming

Do not attempt to cut your chinchilla's teeth yourself unless you have been shown how to do this by your vet and are confident that you can follow her instructions. Otherwise, you could make the situation worse.

If you trim your pet's teeth at home, you'll need a suitable pair of clippers for the task. Scissors should never be used because they will not be strong enough to cut through the tooth. Also, their size is not appropriate, simply because you can inflict injury trying to use them directly in front of your squirmy chinchilla's face.

"Slobbers"

Another sign of a dental problem is wet fur around the mouth, a condition sometimes described as "slobbers." This occurs because of an increased output of saliva, which then dribbles out of the mouth.

The condition may be a reflection of a problem with the molar teeth lying farther back toward the throat. They have raised areas on them known as cusps, not unlike our own molars. Chinchillas use these teeth to chew up food, with the result that they are subjected to considerable wear. Occasionally, though, a raised area called a spur may develop if the wear on the teeth is not even, causing the chinchilla to alter his eating pattern. This in turn allows the spur to worsen because the affected part of the tooth is no longer being worn down.

In such cases, your vet will need to examine the teeth carefully, and this is likely to mean anaesthetising your pet. It will then be possible to remove the spur, although there is a possibility that it could recur.

The presence of a tooth spur may be a sign that your pet does not have access to enough blocks for gnawing purposes, so check on this aspect of your pet's care. If necessary, provide different types of blocks in case your chinchilla is reluctant to sample the ones you have provided previously. As with food, it can sometimes be harder to persuade an older chinchilla to adapt in this respect, but if necessary, offer safe branches that he will almost instinctively chew on; these can be highly beneficial in terms of dental care.

Nail Care

Chinchillas, unlike many other rodents, do not have long nails on their toes. Pedicures are therefore unnecessary because there is little risk of these animals becoming caught up in their quarters by overgrown claws. You do need to be careful that they do

Grooming for Good Health

A regular grooming routine can help you maintain your pet's health and appearance. When you groom your chinchilla, take time to inspect his body and overall condition:

- Monitor his weight: Does he feel too thin, too fat, or just right?

- Examine your pet's coat and body: Are there any bald spots or any unusual lumps or bumps since you last groomed him?

- Check his teeth: Are they in good condition, or are they overgrown?

- Check his eyes, ears, and nose: Does he have discharge from any or all of them?

Knowing what's normal for your pet and noticing changes in his appearance and routine are the first steps in maintaining his health. If you find something unusual, contact your veterinarian. It's much easier to treat minor problems before they become serious health issues.

not become caught up by their feet, however, which will result in injury either to their toes or to their actual limbs.

The nails themselves are kept trim as the chinchilla moves around his quarters. Just check occasionally that there are no sore areas where the nail bed and toe meet, which can be the site of an infection. Injury can occur easily if there are any sharp projections in the chinchilla's quarters as he clambers around because he uses the tips of his front feet to grasp onto objects. If your pet does sustain an injury, he will be reluctant to grip with the affected foot. There also will be an evident swelling on the affected digit. If this occurs, take your chin to the vet for proper treatment.

Ear Care

One of the most conspicuous features of chinchillas is their large ears, which are quite open at their base. Their large size traps sound well and enables chinchillas to pinpoint the location of a noise, triangulate their position, and detect possible danger in their environment. Keen hearing is

also important because chinchillas are quite vocal rodents who keep in touch with each other through a range of different calls.

Luckily, their ears rarely need any attention. On rare occasions, the relatively thin ear flap might become torn if two individuals have a disagreement, but this is uncommon. Minor bleeding usually can be stopped by pressing firmly (but not too hard)

Chinchillas, unlike many other rodents, do not have long nails on their toes. Pedicures are therefore unnecessary.

Time spent grooming offers an opportunity to build the bond of trust with your pet.

on the affected area to stimulate clotting. After the injury heals, there may be a small tear evident, but this will not inconvenience the chinchilla to any significant extent.

If you notice that your chinchilla is scratching repeatedly at one of his ears, this may suggest that something has entered the ear canal and is causing an irritation there. Do not be tempted to probe down into the ear canal yourself because this could force the foreign body farther down into the ear, where

it will be harder to retrieve. Instead, seek veterinary care. It should be relatively easy for your vet to retrieve any object or correct any problem because she has special equipment available for this purpose, causing your chinchilla only minimal distress.

Eye Care

Although large and prominent, a chinchilla's eyes need little in the way of grooming. However, if your chinchilla is suffering from weepy eyes, this could be the result of a small piece of hay or even dusting powder entering the eye. This can happen quite easily on occasion because the eye surface is so large and as such is constantly exposed to all of the interior components of the cage.

A foreign object in the affected eye will increase tear fluid production, leading to the fur at the corner of the eye becoming wet. This may be self-limiting, with the increased tear fluid washing out the debris. But if it persists, there may be another cause, such as the roots of the incisor teeth exerting pressure. Your vet can confirm the source of the problem and treat it.

A Time to Bond

Regular grooming can help with the taming process, especially with a young chinchilla. It also helps to strengthen the bond between you and your pet. Because these small creatures are so affectionate and cuddly, it won't be hard for you to find time to spoil your chinchilla with some regular pampering. Both you and your pet will be the better for it!

FAMILY-FRIENDLY TIP

Grooming Sessions for Kids

With adult supervision, a child can help with grooming chores by gently restraining the chinchilla or combing his coat while you hold your pet. Older children can help by preparing the dust bath once they have seen how much powder is required. They can also watch over the chinchilla as he bathes. Afterward, they can assist in the cleanup by removing the bath container and cleaning and storing all of the grooming supplies so that they will be ready for the next grooming session.

63

Looking Good

Chapter 5

Feeling Good

Chinchillas are usually healthy animals who rarely require veterinary attention, as long as their nutritional and housing needs are adequately met. Be alert to signs of illness, however, so that if necessary, you can seek the advice of a veterinarian without delay. The earlier treatment begins, the greater your chinchilla's chances of a full recovery. This, as much as the medication itself, can be a major factor affecting the outcome of your pet's illness because his condition is likely to deteriorate rapidly if left untreated.

Finding a Vet

Although your chinchilla may never need veterinary care, it is still important to know which practice in your area to consult in the case of an emergency. Some veterinarians have more experience with small animals than others, and this is particularly so with chinchillas. It may be worthwhile to call several veterinary practices in your area to inquire if one or more of the veterinarians has particular expertise in this field. Alternatively, if you purchased your chinchilla from a breeder in your locality, ask which veterinarian they would recommend based on their experience.

Even if you cannot find a veterinarian locally who deals extensively with small animal patients, don't worry. All veterinarians undergo rigorous training and will be able to assist if your chinchilla does fall ill, even to the extent of being able to seek advice from colleagues with more expertise in a particular area if required.

Young chinchillas do not need any routine shots, unlike puppies or kittens. Assuming that your chin appears healthy, it's not necessary to get an initial vet check after purchase, but

Your chinchilla is dependent on you for his good health and well-being.

it's usually a good idea to do so if only to be certain that all is in order and to establish a relationship with the veterinarian you have decided to use.

Bear in mind that a chinchilla is most likely to fall ill during his first few weeks with you. This is not a reflection on your lack of experience if you have not kept a chinchilla before. Rather, it reflects the way in which animals moved to new surroundings encounter different bacteria and similar microbes to which they have less resistance. In addition, they are likely to have suffered a degree of stress following their move, which in turn may have lowered their resistance to disease. Young chinchillas are particularly vulnerable because their immune systems are unlikely to be as effective when confronted by potential disease-causing microbes as those of older animals.

The Adjustment Period

There are a number of things that you can do to prevent your chinchilla from falling ill during this initial period with you. First, do not take a chinchilla home with you unless you are certain that he has been fully weaned and is quite able to feed himself. Obtain a diet sheet when you collect your pet, and follow it carefully to minimise the risk of any digestive upset, which could have serious consequences. Find out in advance what type of food your chinchilla is eating and obtain a supply of it before obtaining your pet so that there will be no need to offer an unfamiliar food. Also, although they

FAMILY-FRIENDLY TIP

Preparing a Child for a Vet Visit

Children can learn a lot about the family pet and his proper care by accompanying you when you bring your pet to the vet. Preparing your children for what will happen at the vet's surgery will make the experience less stressful. Depending on their age and level of understanding, you can explain why your chinchilla needs to see the vet (or "chinchilla doctor") even if the animal isn't sick. Explain that you will get to the vet's surgery and need to check in before the exam. You also must tell them that it is very important to sit quietly to avoid frightening the chinchilla while he is being examined. Children need to realise that their pet will be rather frightened, and they must not make any noise that will upset him.

Ask the vet to explain each step of the process during the checkup. If a child has questions about the chinchilla's general behaviour or health care routine, encourage him or her to ask the vet directly. Most are happy to answer questions from children and are pleased to see them taking a responsible role in pet care.

Feeling Good

may help with the taming process later on, do not offer too many treats of different types to your new chinchilla.

Aside from your pet's diet, keep his surroundings clean to guard against possible infections. Food and water containers need to be washed regularly, and it is also important that you wash your hands before offering food or handling your chinchilla. Bacteria such as *E. coli* that we may carry on our bodies could threaten a chinchilla's health. The risk is greatest if you are preparing fresh food that needs to be handled and cut up. Always do this immediately before feeding your pet, rather than leaving the food sitting around before it is required. Bacteria like *E.coli* can double their numbers every

20 minutes or so, which means that the danger from contaminated food is rapidly magnified as a result, especially if it is prepared and left uneaten for any amount of time.

Always allow a short period of time every day to spend time with your chinchilla, especially during an adjustment period. Aside from needing social interaction with you, this will hopefully allow you to recognise if your pet is showing any signs of illness at a relatively early stage. Should you be concerned at all, contact your veterinarian immediately. The likelihood of your pet making a full recovery will be greatly increased as a result because small animals may not show signs of illness until the condition has already become serious.

Although your chinchilla may never need veterinary care, it is still important to know which practice in your area to consult in the case of an emergency.

The Vet Visit

If you need to take your pet to the vet for any reason, transfer him to a suitable, secure carrier. Take him directly to the clinic, and never leave him unattended in any vehicle. Even on a moderately warm day, the temperature is likely to rise to a fatal level very quickly, which is dangerous given the chinchilla's susceptibility to heatstroke. If necessary, keep the air conditioning on for the duration of the trip to avoid stressing your chinchilla unnecessarily. Be wary of opening any windows, though, as this could cause your pet to be exposed to a draft.

It will be safest to fit the carrier either on the floor of the vehicle in the front foot well or on the floor behind the front seats. Here, the carrier will be relatively secure and unlikely to be tipped over, even if you brake suddenly in an emergency. Position the carrier in such a way that your chinchilla cannot reach through the mesh and cause any damage to the fabric in your car. Although it is not essential for a short journey, you can attach a water bottle to the front door of the cage in case your chinchilla needs a drink. This is especially important if your pet is suffering from dehydration as the result of diarrhoea.

When you arrive at your vet's surgery, check in, or possibly register officially if you have not attended the clinic before. When you are waiting for the consultation, keep your chinchilla's carrier off the ground so that he isn't frightened by other pets that may be in the surgery at the same time; most dogs

When Veterinary Care Is a Must

In the case of chinchillas, it is always important not to delay in seeking veterinary help. Because of his small size, the condition of a sick chinchilla can worsen rapidly. Any of the following signs are indicative that veterinary assistance is necessary:

- ongoing diarrhoea
- loss of appetite
- prolonged inactivity, often linked with an unusual body posture
- mobility problems

69

will be keen to investigate what is in the carrier. Try to sit in a quiet corner of the waiting room rather than by the door if possible.

Expect to be asked some general questions by the vet, such as how long you have had your pet, what he is eating, and whether he lives with any other chinchillas, and if so, if they appear healthy. You also will need to explain what is worrying you about your pet's health. Your vet will then want to examine the chinchilla, having established his clinical history. You may be expected to hold your pet while

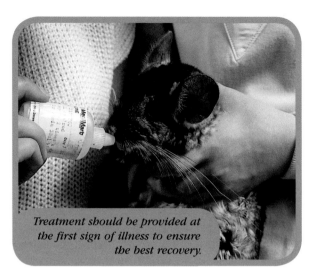
Treatment should be provided at the first sign of illness to ensure the best recovery.

the vet looks more closely for signs of loss of body condition or more specific problems such as staining around the vent area, which is common in cases of diarrhoea.

There are also a number of tests that can be carried out, depending on the cause of your concern. If there is likely to be a possible infection, or in the case of heatstroke, your vet may take your pet's temperature. It should normally be between 100° to 101°F (37.8° to 38.3°C). Faecal sampling may be indicated in the case of a digestive upset, while skin scrapings might be indicated in the case of unexplained loss of coat. An ever more sophisticated array of clinical tests, often using blood samples, are available as well. This means that it can be easier to determine the source of the problem more reliably now than in the past, particularly as knowledge about veterinary problems in chinchillas and

their treatment has also increased significantly.

Signs of Illness

There are likely to be several clues in your chin's environment that indicate he is not well, starting with the amount of food being consumed. He may eat less than usual because a sick chinchilla will normally lose his appetite. You also may notice a change in the appearance of his droppings. When ill, a chinchilla is often likely to be sleepier. Do bear in mind, however, that chinchillas will normally sleep throughout the day, so this is quite normal.

You soon will become familiar with your pet's cycle of activity and able to notice if there is any divergence in it that indicates a cause for concern. This applies particularly if your chinchilla also adopts a different posture, appears hunched up, or if his fur is lying flatter than usual, which may reveal that he has not been dust bathing as much as normal.

It is often quite easy to determine that a chinchilla is ill but much harder to identify the cause of the illness, which is essential to administering effective treatment. This is where your veterinarian will be able to help.

Common Health Problems

Experienced pet owners and breeders are adept at recognising when a pet is sick. As you gain experience caring for your pet, especially if you develop a long-term interest, you also will become more proficient at it. Sick chinchillas generally will present a similar range of symptoms.

Digestive Disorders

The rhythm of the intestinal tract is important in ensuring that a chinchilla can obtain maximum benefit from his food. If food passes too quickly through the intestinal tract, with the so-called "passage time" speeded up accordingly, the result is diarrhoea. Conversely, if it slows down, constipation results.

It is actually not uncommon for an episode of diarrhoea to be followed by a period of constipation. This is partly because diarrhoea results in fluid loss to the extent that the animal will be at risk of dehydration, which is in turn a cause of constipation. It is also a reflection of the fact that the rhythm of the normal peristaltic contractions of the gut that move the food along have been disturbed. Constipation resulting from diarrhoea should resolve itself naturally, provided that the chinchilla has adequate fibre in the form of hay still available. A small amount of greens also can act as a laxative under these conditions.

The most common cause of diarrhoea in chinchillas is probably unsuitable food or feeding, with other contributory factors involved on occasion too, including stress. The altered conditions in the intestinal tract then make it much easier for this part of the body to be colonised by harmful bacteria, resulting in a full-blown infection that endangers the chinchilla's life. Diarrhoea is therefore a condition that requires rapid veterinary treatment in the hope that it can be contained, although a long-standing way of attempting to counter diarrhoea in the absence of any antibiotic treatment is to provide the affected chinchilla with pieces of dry toast.

A major difficulty with this problem is that it can be problematic to use antibiotics to treat an infection satisfactorily because of the chinchilla's reliance on beneficial bacteria to aid the digestion of his food. What can easily happen is that the antibiotic helps to eliminate the harmful bacteria, but in so doing, destroys a significant

Stick to the Right Medication

In the case of a chinchilla suffering from diarrhoea, never be tempted to use over-the-counter products available to treat people with this condition. They are probably completely unsuitable and could easily cause serious and potentially life-threatening complications to a small pet. Only use medication as advised by your veterinarian to treat diarrhoea or any other illness. In some cases, tests may be necessary to see if your pet is suffering from internal parasites, especially if he suffers from recurrent diarrhoea, which may suggest that the regular treatment is not working.

number of the beneficial population as well. This then interferes with the digestive process, although now specific probiotics may be used to overcome the worst effects of antibiotic treatment. A probiotic contains beneficial bacteria and effectively helps either to reseed the gut after a course of antibiotics, or these bacteria serve to create favourable conditions for the existing beneficial bacteria to repopulate the intestinal tract, effectively preventing colonisation by potentially harmful species.

Eye Ailments

A chinchilla's eyes may often be vulnerable to injury because they spend time sleeping near shavings and taking dust baths. For example, a scratch to the eye surface caused by a piece of hay or dust can trigger an irritation if not an infection.

If your pet is suffering from an eye ailment, your veterinarian may prescribe medication either in the form of drops or an ointment that you need to give your pet on a regular basis, typically about four times throughout the course of the day. Ointment is

Emergency Preparedness

Although you need to seek veterinary advice before taking any action in an emergency, there are certain things that may be useful to have at home in case a medical problem or injury befalls your chinchilla. You might already have a number of these items at home. They include:

- cotton balls and swabs for wiping your pet's ears or cleaning any wounds
- styptic powder or a styptic pencil that can be applied to a minor injury to stimulate the clotting process
- a small clean towel that you can soak if necessary should your pet develop heatstroke
- a rectal thermometer for taking your chinchilla's temperature, plus a suitable lubricant jelly
- a suitable ophthalmic ointment for minor eye ailments
- an antiseptic solution like hydrogen peroxide, iodine, or rubbing alcohol to disinfect and treat wounds
- gauze pads, self-adhering bandage material, first-aid tape, scissors, and tweezers for treating and dressing wounds

Also, keep contact info for your vet where it can be accessed easily at all times.

An unusual change in your chinchilla's behaviour, appearance, or mood may indicate that he is ill.

perhaps easier to apply because if the chinchilla blinks at the wrong moment, the drop may not even enter the eye. Using ointment, however, means that you will need to hold your pet for a few minutes so that ointment dissolves into the eye rather than being wiped off by his paw.

Frequent treatment is vital to your pet's recovery. This is because the increased output of tear fluid linked with any infection will wash the medication out of the eye, reducing its effectiveness more rapidly than normal. It is therefore important to keep treating the affected eye as instructed to maintain a therapeutic level of the drug in your pet's system. Eye ailments

often can heal quite rapidly, but always complete the course of treatment to be certain that the infection is eliminated.

Cuts and Scrapes

Although chinchillas normally live together happily, there are times when they may disagree quite violently with each other. This is most common in the case of individuals who have recently been introduced to each other as adults, so supervise them closely at first under these circumstances. Two males are particularly likely to fight, and the result can be serious. A chinchilla's prominent ears are especially vulnerable to being injured, but there also may be other wounds that are less evident on the limbs or body.

The risk with such wounds is not just the immediate loss of blood and associated stress, but also the threat of a possible infection developing at the site of the injury. Start by bathing the wound with a clean cotton ball. There is little point in trying to bandage it in any way because the dressing is soon likely to be removed by your chinchilla. Hopefully, it should stop bleeding quickly, especially if you apply a styptic powder or pencil to the wound.

If you suspect that the injury is not healing properly, consult your vet. A topical antibiotic that can be applied to the infected area is often sufficient to overcome this problem without having to try a more generalised course of antibiotic therapy. Obviously, it is also important that your chinchillas are not placed back in the same enclosure.

Fur Problems

Although chinchillas do not suffer from skin parasites, thanks to their dense fur, this does not protect them entirely from infections on the surface of the body. Therefore, always be alert to any areas of hair loss because these will need to be investigated. For example, there is a possibility that your pet might have acquired ringworm, which is a relatively serious condition that can be transmitted to people. The fungal spores themselves may have been introduced on the hay he has been fed. Alternatively, especially if you have a cat, you may have inadvertently spread the illness while petting another pet

Excessive Handling

The quality of the fur may be affected by how much you and other family members handle your chinchilla. Excessive handling will cause the fur to appear flat, often with a greasy texture. Try to restrict handling sessions under these circumstances, which should hopefully lead to a rapid improvement in your pet's condition.

and then picking up your chinchilla without washing your hands.

Some strains of ringworm can be diagnosed easily. If the area of hair loss is examined in a darkened environment at the vet's surgery using a special lamp, the affected area will appear bright fluorescent green. When there is no fluorescence, however, and ringworm is suspected, skin scrapings may need to be taken to see if a fungus is present; the spores will grow in the laboratory on special media. This is a much slower process, and it may take several weeks to obtain a definitive diagnosis. It is actually the outer edge at the site of infection rather than the central area where the hair has been lost that will have the highest concentration of fungal spores present.

A prescribed topical treatment applied to the affected area in the form of a cream will be necessary. You can use a cotton swab for this purpose so that you don't have to rub the ointment directly into the affected area, although you should wear disposable gloves as a precautionary measure in any case. Ringworm in people usually manifests itself on the forearms, where the skin is most likely to have been in contact with the chinchilla's fur. Infected areas will appear as red circular patches. If you develop this condition, obtain medical advice and treatment.

The fungal spores that are responsible for ringworm are persistent in the environment. You will need to disinfect your pet's quarters thoroughly, as recommended by your veterinarian, in addition to using the cream. Be patient because it will take several weeks for this treatment to be effective. In the meantime, only handle your pet with gloves, and wear long sleeves to reduce the risk of acquiring the fungal spores yourself. The chance that your chinchilla will develop ringworm is slight, however, so do not be unduly worried by this possibility.

Fur Chewing

A far more common cause of fur damage in chinchillas is chewing of the coat, either by the affected individual or a companion. There are a number of potential causes in such cases, and it is not always easy to unravel the underlying reason, particularly because there may be more than one contributing factor involved. Unfortunately, it is also not easy to spot whether the chinchilla is mutilating himself or the loss of fur is being inflicted by a companion, which often occurs at night or in the nest box.

The simplest way to investigate this is to separate your chinchillas to see if the fur loss continues, in which case, it was not the chinchilla's companion who was the cause of the problem. On the other hand, just to show how difficult it is to investigate what is essentially a stress-related problem, it might have been the proximity of a companion that caused the chinchilla to start pulling out his own fur!

Overcrowding is frequently a cause of this behaviour. It is sometimes described as "barbering." Being in crowded quarters is especially likely to be the source of fur chewing if you have recently introduced a new chinchilla to your established pet. It may be a sign that they are not getting along well. Suspect this as a likely

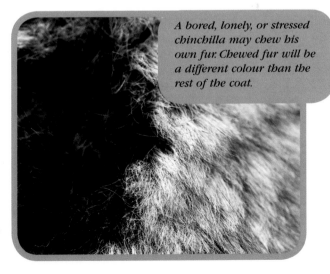

A bored, lonely, or stressed chinchilla may chew his own fur. Chewed fur will be a different colour than the rest of the coat.

First Aid

In spite of your best attempts to provide a safe environment, there can be times when a chinchilla injures himself, either within his quarters or when out in a room. Young chinchillas are especially at risk for injury because of their lively natures. The way that you deal with this type of situation depends partly on the actual nature of the injury and what you have available to treat it. As a general rule, it is safest to seek veterinary advice without delay. However, if your pet has a bad wound, the first thing you should do is to place him in his carrier and cover it with a cloth to create a darkened environment where he may calm down. Once settled, make your trip to the vet, ensuring that he is secure and that the wound has been temporarily treated and any bleeding stemmed as much as possible.

a larger cage is recommended, but some individuals simply prove to be less compatible than others. The only long-term solution is to separate them permanently, although this does not mean that they will be compatible with other individuals either.

Environmental triggers also can cause this type of behaviour. For example, sleep deprivation may result in stress-motivated chewing. Any loud noises near your chinchilla's quarters, particularly if they are repeated constantly throughout the day, can have this effect. This is why it is never a good idea to house your chinchilla near highly trafficked areas or near a television or a stereo system, especially if you like listening to loud rock music. Construction involving a lot of banging and dust in the atmosphere that continues over several weeks could be upsetting as well.

The introduction of a new pet such as a cat also might be a worry if the animal ends up sitting on top of your chinchilla's quarters or stalking him around the sides of his enclosure all the time. If you are to have any hope of resolving the problem, other household pets must be kept out of the room where your chinchilla is being kept.

When stress is the cause, it will take some time for hair to regrow, depending on what particular stage in the chinchilla's shedding cycle has been reached. It will, however, regrow spontaneously because damaged hair will be replaced by new strands. Should you find that this does not occur, the situation is clearly more serious.

cause if only one of the chinchillas uses the nest box and the other is sleeping on the floor. Unfortunately, resolving this problem can be difficult. Obtaining

Environmental conditions like excessive heat, overcrowding, or toxic fumes are unhealthy for your pet.

Unfortunately, it may be that the behaviour has become habitual, and breaking the cycle may be impossible. This is why it is so important to try to identify the initial cause without delay at the outset.

Pica

There can be many other potential causes of hair loss. You may want to write down things that have been happening in the home in the preceding weeks because this sometimes can help to identify something that you may have overlooked. Perhaps you changed your chinchilla's dusting powder or bedding, or you ran short of hay and neglected to provide as much as usual. Things of this sort can trigger hair loss for a different reason.

A shortage of fibre in the diet sometimes causes a chinchilla to seek alternative sources in his environment, and as a result, he starts to eat his own fur. "Pica" is the term used to describe a chinchilla's abnormal desire to behave in this way. Correcting the diet in this case should be sufficient to resolve the problem.

A change in bedding can be harder to pinpoint as the cause, but there could be some type of allergen causing irritation, particularly if it is the fur on

Unplanned Pregnancy

Chinchillas usually become capable of reproduction from the age of around 4 to 6 months, depending on the individual, of course. Female chinchillas can become pregnant as young as 5-1/2 months old. Male chinchillas can begin impregnating females when as young as 4 months. Usually, you will see a white deposit of material known as a copulatory plug in their quarters, which confirms that mating has taken place. If this was successful, the female has a long period of pregnancy, lasting for about 111 days. She will need more food, especially toward the end of her pregnancy and while she is suckling her young.

Should mating have occurred, there is little that can be done to stop the female having kits, but at least, unlike many rodents, chinchillas only have small litters comprising anywhere from one to four offspring. They normally will be born within a period of two or three hours, usually at night, and are fully developed at birth. They will need to remain with their mother for up to eight weeks, and you must be careful when weaning them. Restrict the quantity of pellets offered to them at this stage to prevent diarrhoea.

As soon as you realise that mating has taken place, separate the pair, allowing the female to have the young on her own. Keep the chinchillas apart in the future to prevent unwanted litters, or discuss neutering one of your pets with your veterinarian.

the lower body that is being nibbled. If you are concerned, try reverting to your original hay supply if it is still available, or seek out fresh bedding elsewhere.

Be very careful when using sprays of any kind around the home, particularly in the room where your chinchilla is housed. They could potentially cause irritation, with your pet scratching determinedly at his fur before starting to chew the strands of hair. Where scratching is stress-induced, however, your chinchilla will not show such signs of discomfort but will instead simply damage the fur. Eliminating irritants may provide a vital means of distinguishing between these possible causes.

Fractures

Chinchillas occasionally can suffer fractures, often of their hind legs, as the result of a fall. For this reason,

never encourage your pet to climb onto high shelves. If your pet does fall and suffers a fracture under these circumstances, he is likely to be in obvious discomfort and unable to move freely. Avoid handling your chinchilla more than strictly necessary under these circumstances, simply because shock is likely to develop and can prove fatal in some cases. It is much better simply to confine your chinchilla to his carrier and arrange to take him to your vet. Your chinchilla can be x-rayed to determine the extent of the injury and treated, although it is not easy to keep a dressing or cast on for long because he will try to remove it. If the fracture can be stabilised, there is every chance that your pet will make a good recovery.

Poisoning

It can be surprisingly difficult to diagnose poisoning in chinchillas with

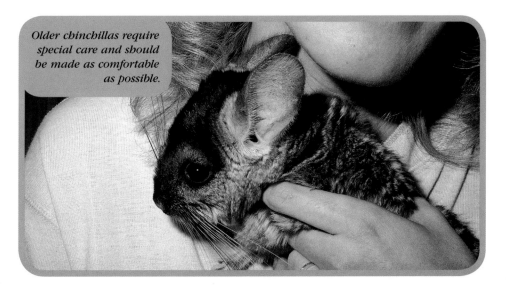

Older chinchillas require special care and should be made as comfortable as possible.

With proper care, your chinchilla can live for 15 years or more.

certainty because it need not just be something that your pet has eaten. The poison could be something in the environment in the form of a chemical spray, for example. Cigarette or cigar smoke could also cause problems for your pet. So at the very least, avoid smoking in the same room where your chinchilla is being housed.

Stress

Stress can be a killer, especially in the case of chinchillas. There are different forms of stress, but basically, this condition can be defined as anything that exerts a harmful effect on the body's processes. It can result from the increased heart rate that accompanies fear or the inability of a chinchilla to lower his body temperature when confronted by excessive heat. Treating stress involves removing the cause of the problem and allowing the body's internal mechanisms that have been affected to return to normal.

Signs of stress are directly related to the cause. Heat stress causes chinchillas to lie in such a way as to try to cool down, and this is one situation where you will need to wrap your chinchilla in a towel soaked in cold (but not freezing) water, or even carefully submerge his body in a bowl of water for a few moments, ensuring that your pet is not at risk of drowning. If this doesn't help, a trip to the vet is urgent.

Senior Care

As chinchillas grow older, they can suffer from a range of minor health problems that affect their quality of life. Although you will not be able to turn back the clock, there are certain things that you can do to make life easier for your pet at this stage of his life.

The first thing you may notice is that your chinchilla will gradually become less lively. Because this change occurs over time, it may not be that conspicuous, but try redesigning your pet's quarters slightly so that it's easier for him to climb around. Older chinchillas also will be less able to regulate their body temperature effectively, so they will be susceptible to heatstroke. You may need to reassess where you place your pet's quarters in the home to be sure that an elderly chinchilla is less likely to be exposed to any significant variances in temperature.

A senior's vision will become less acute with age. Older chins also tend to develop cataracts. These will be apparent as whitish opaque areas over the surface of the eyes. Luckily, though, because they are normally active in a nocturnal world, chinchillas rely far less on their eyesight than we do, especially when compared with their other senses. Waning vision, therefore,

will not affect them greatly, although it might cause misjudgment if they need to jump, increasing the associated risk of injury. Nevertheless, cataracts are not routinely treated in elderly chinchillas.

Keep a closer watch than previously on your pet's teeth if he is more than ten years of age because there is an increasing risk that they will become overgrown and need to be trimmed back. Also, they may change colour from a healthy yellow to white. This could possibly be an indication of underlying kidney failure, particularly if combined with weight loss.

Chinchillas also can suffer from some of the age-related illnesses that we do, such as problems of the cardiovascular system, kidney and liver failure, arthritis, etc. The signs of these illnesses may not be immediately evident, although they may show up as part of a routine medical exam carried out by your veterinarian. There is usually nothing that can be done by way of treatment in such cases, but provided that your chinchilla is not unduly stressed and made as comfortable as possible, he may be able to live with some of these problems for a while.

Chapter 6

Being Good

One of the great things about having a chinchilla as a pet is the way in which these rodents can be very easily tamed. This is an important part of ownership because there will be times when you will need to be able to pick up or restrain your chinchilla. In addition, it means that you will be able to let your pet out into the room for regular periods of exercise, knowing that he won't be too difficult to catch again when necessary. Taming him also provides an opportunity to strengthen the bond between you and your pet.

Handling and Taming

Like all rodents, chinchillas have an understandably nervous disposition, which literally can save their lives in the wild because it allows them to flee rapidly at the approach of a would-be predator. With patience, however, you will be able to break down this barrier and tame your new pet, especially if you start with a young chinchilla. They have far less fear at an early age compared to an older chinchilla, especially one who has never been handled.

Taming is not difficult, but it will require patience on your part. It is also important not to make sudden movements that will scare your pet. In addition, noises elsewhere in the home, such as a door slamming, may well cause the chinchilla to retreat back inside his nest box or to another part of his cage where he feels secure. If this happens when the chinchilla is free in the room, he will seek to hide somewhere nearby, possibly darting behind a piece of furniture. These rodents have acute hearing, relying heavily on this sense to protect them from danger.

The Taming Process

If you are starting out with a young chinchilla who has recently been weaned, it should be quite easy to win his confidence, although it is not something that can be achieved instantly. You may need to explain this to younger members of the household who are likely to be anxious to handle their new companion. Put this in a way that they will understand, perhaps by saying that the young chinchilla is frightened being away from his mother

With patience and consistency, chinchillas can be easily tamed.

and will need time to adjust to his new home.

To begin the taming process, sit alongside your chinchilla's cage and talk to him. Try offering him a treat such as a piece of carrot. It should be cut into a thin strip so that you can offer it by holding it at one end. Keep your hand still, and gently encourage your chinchilla to take the food from your fingers. If he ignores it at first, be patient. Speak slowly and softly, giving encouragement, which also will help him become used to the sound of your voice.

Do not be tempted to wave the piece of carrot around as a way of attracting his attention. This will just scare him. At first, you are likely to find that your chinchilla may cautiously sniff the carrot and retreat rather than taking it from your hand. Such behaviour is normal. If you have to end the taming session, simply leave the carrot in the same place in which you were offering it.

When you come back, you are likely to find that he has picked the treat up and carried it away, or even eaten it on the spot. Bear in mind, too, that thanks to their nocturnal lifestyles, chinchillas are most likely to emerge from their retreats in search of food from late afternoon onward, and this is therefore the best time to encourage them to feed from your hand. Once a chinchilla does take a treat from your hand, simply let it slide out of your fingers and wait until he has backed off with his prize before moving your hand. Otherwise, you are likely to find

FAMILY-FRIENDLY TIP

Teaching a Child Proper Handling

The best way to teach your child how to handle a chinchilla correctly is simply by way of example. Start by picking up the chinchilla yourself, and allow your pet to roam free in the room for a short period. Be sure that you have pet-proofed the area before allowing your pet out of his enclosure, however. Then catch the chinchilla, and encourage your child to take him from you gently, preferably when she is sitting down. Children will otherwise tend to hold a chinchilla too tightly for fear of dropping the animal when standing up. Proper handling and taming are things that they can only learn through experience and specific instruction from the pet's caretakers.

A child of 6 or 7 can be allowed to pet a chinchilla, although it is probably not a good idea to allow children under 10 to handle one on their own. You must always supervise all interactions with pets and consistently stress that repeated handling can stress the pet.

that your pet simply drops the treat, becoming scared by your sudden movement.

Training Treats

Treats are a great motivational tool and one of the best things you can use to help in taming or training your pet if used in moderation.

Larger treats such as a dandelion leaf or a piece of carrot are ideal for taming a reluctant chinchilla because they are more easily handled. Once your pet is feeding readily from your hand, start to offer smaller items such as raisins. There are also healthy commercial treats made specifically for chinchillas that you can buy, and these need to be offered as recommended on the packaging. Do not offer treats intended for other small pets as they may make your chinchilla ill.

Another advantage to offering treats is that they can be used to lure your pet out of a hiding place or to coax him into doing something you want him to do; they work as positive reinforcement when your pet performs as you ask. Also, by rewarding your pet's good behaviour with food initially, you make him more likely to repeat the behaviour.

Once your pet is behaving well, however, try to alternate food with verbal praise or cuddling to ensure that he won't become overweight from consuming too many goodies.

One of the most important aspects of taming your chinchilla is to offer a treat in this way every day around the same time. In fact, you are likely to find that he soon comes to anticipate the treat and will be waiting for you as a result. This is great way to build up a bond between you, but it is also a good way to monitor your pet's health. If you notice one day that he is not keen to come and take his treat, this can be an early warning sign of possible illness, which will need to be investigated.

Picking Up Your Chinchilla

As we have already established, one of the most important things when it comes to taming a chinchilla is to develop a routine. The same will apply when you want to get him accustomed to being handled. By allowing your pet out of his quarters regularly at the same time, he will begin to anticipate this period to explore the room every day.

Some new owners may be concerned about being nipped when first attempting to handle their pet. Although chinchillas do have sharp teeth that can inflict a painful bite, an individual is unlikely to react in this way when picked up. You are more likely to be bitten by accident when offering a treat if the chinchilla keeps munching the food being held in your fingers.

There are certain things you can do to make it much easier to pick up your chinchilla. First, speak quietly to him because this will provide reassurance and should make him less inclined to struggle. Bear in mind that chinchillas equate being held tightly with being seized by a predator. Although you must restrain your pet properly when picking him up, do not aim to overpower him. You just want to ensure that he cannot wriggle free and fall to the floor, which could result in an injury as serious as a fractured limb.

At first, it is likely to be much harder to catch your chinchilla. He will not be used to this experience and will be fearful, moving around the cage quickly to elude your grasp. Try to carry out the catching process with minimal disturbance. It may even help if you simply take your chinchilla out of his nest box, choosing a time immediately before he would normally wake up. A chinchilla will soon become used to being roused from his slumbers in this way and will not resent the intrusion.

When you pick up a chinchilla, scoop him up from beneath. To begin, place your hands on each side of the body to slow him down so that he doesn't try to run away. Then gently slide your hand under his body just behind the front legs. Next, shift your other hand more centrally

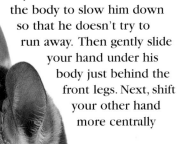

Begin taming by hand-feeding your pet. This establishes trust and encourages him to accept handling later on.

No Shouting!

If your chinchilla starts doing something that could be harmful when allowed out into a room, do not start shouting at him or scolding him because he will not comprehend that he has done something wrong. Simply remove him from harm's way and try to alter the environment so that the situation will not arise again. Shouting can cause your chinchilla considerable distress because of the sensitivity of his hearing.

over your pet's back so that you can lift him up safely, providing adequate support beneath the body, especially around the heavier rear end. This is important because if a chinchilla feels uncomfortable and thinks that he is likely to slip out of your hand, he will struggle and become more likely to do so.

Out and About

Although you should always transfer a chinchilla to a carrier if you intend to venture outside, taking your pet to the vet for example, it should be safe to move a tame chinchilla around the room by carrying him in this way.

It is probably not a good idea to go up stairs carrying your pet though, because if you are distracted, even momentarily, you may drop him from a greater height than would otherwise be the case.

When your chinchilla is first allowed out of his enclosure and into the room, you are likely to find that he runs around quite wildly after initially pausing to seek cover. If you have a pair of chinchillas living together, it will be better to allow them out individually so that you can supervise them more closely. Otherwise, while you are watching one pet, the other could easily disappear and end up injured out of your sight elsewhere in the room.

Before expecting your chinchilla to sit with you, allow him to burn off energy by having a run around the room right after he has been let out of his quarters. This should ensure that your pet will be more relaxed. Some chinchillas are more willing to sit alongside their owners than others. Again, if you start with a young chinchilla, you are more likely to find that he will be easier to persuade than an adult who has little or no experience with human contact. This can be a problem with rescue chinchillas, so more patience will be needed in such cases.

Once your chinchilla is sitting alongside you, offer him a treat to encourage him to remain there, although, as usual, it is vital not to overindulge him with too many treats at any stage. Some chinchillas like being petted more than others. It may be a question of gently stroking your pet's head to see how he reacts. Assuming that he accepts it, you can then start to stroke him down his back.

The length of time that is required to tame a chinchilla depends on a number of factors, not the least being how friendly your pet is at the outset. Individual chinchillas actually do seem to differ in their acceptance of human company. Another significant factor is how much time you can spend with your pet. It is much better to be able to spend a shorter time every evening taming your chinchilla rather than just having a marathon session on the weekend.

Remember, too, that chinchillas react to a number of different stimuli. Therefore, in addition to watching your movements, a chinchilla will be particularly influenced by the sounds you make. This is significant because they are relatively vocal themselves. Although your chinchilla will not be able to learn his name, he will come to recognise certain sounds and realise that they have a pleasant meaning, which will help him overcome any fear that he may have during early stages of taming.

Free Roaming

Chinchillas are curious, lively animals who will undoubtedly benefit from being allowed out of their enclosure to exercise. However, there are certain safeguards that you need to put into place first. Start by checking the safety aspects within the designated room, bearing in mind that chinchillas are not only very nimble, but they also can inflict damage with their sharp teeth.

Before letting your chinchilla out of his enclosure, make sure the room is pet-proofed and inform other family members that he will be roaming about.

Keeping Your Pet Safe

Chinchillas may be relatively large rodents, but they are still able to disappear easily within the confines of a room. You therefore need to concentrate on where your pet is at all times whenever he is out of his quarters. Be sure not to wander off, perhaps to answer the telephone, and leave the door open because your chinchilla could follow you rapidly out of the room. The ability of these rodents to hop and jump also means that stairs are no barrier to them, and trying to track down an escapee in the home can prove very worrying, particularly if an outer door has also been open at some stage.

Chinchillas also can get themselves into trouble wandering about the house. They can easily end up under a large, unmovable piece of furniture or get lost in a closet or cabinet, so it's important to have any potential routes to hiding places blocked off before you give your pet out-of-cage time. If your pet escapes and ends up in a place you can't easily reach him, put some of his favourite treats in an open area. Step away from the area in which he's hiding, and call his name sweetly to encourage him to come out. In time, his curiosity and love of treats will likely coax him out of hiding and back into your reach.

If you find that your chinchilla has picked up a power cable and is about to gnaw on it, do not rush over and try to pick up your pet. He might just bite harder into the cable, with deadly consequences. Instead, move quietly to switch off the power to the appliance, and disconnect the plug before approaching him.

Move any valuable objects just in case your pet decides to leap off a chair onto a shelf or chest, knocking over a precious heirloom as a result. Do not leave dangerous plants such as cacti in the room either, in case your chinchilla comes into contact with the spines, and remove those that are likely to be toxic if eaten. These may include many household plants such as ivies and bulbs as well, so it is generally better to remove all plants as a precautionary measure. Open fires

Exercise is not only important for your chinchilla's physical health, it is also necessary for his mental health.

are also potentially hazardous and must be securely and safely screened.

Always go through a ritual before letting your chinchilla out to be certain that the room is safe, and let other people in the home know what you are doing. Take care to ensure that windows and doors are closed so that your pet cannot escape outdoors, where recapturing him could be very difficult. If you have a dog or a cat, keep them from the room before taking your chinchilla out of his cage to protect him from any rough or possibly dangerous encounters. Chinchillas are at much greater risk out of their

cage because other pets are less likely to ignore them. Remember too that cats can sometimes decide to sleep in places hidden from view, so check this out just to be safe.

Also, check for household hazards. Turn off and disconnect power cables to lamps, electronics, and appliances. This will avoid any risk of your chinchilla electrocuting himself if he decides to gnaw on a cable. Try as

much as possible either to remove such appliances to another part of the home or to loop the cabling up where it will be out of reach. Telephone and television cabling can be other hazards and will need to be concealed as much as possible when your chinchilla is free in the room.

Take particular care after you have had your carpets cleaned because some chemicals used in this process may leave residues that might be harmful to the chinchillas. This may show itself in terms of localised hair loss on parts of the body such as the legs or under parts that have been in closest contact with the carpet. Ideally, a tiled or wooden floor is better than a carpeted one, simply because your pet cannot nibble easily at floor coverings of this type and as such will not be at risk of suffering any internal impaction from consuming carpet fibres.

Routine Exercise

Exercise is not only important for your chinchilla's physical health, it is also necessary for his mental health. Try to establish a regular schedule for activity outside of the cage. Set aside time in the evening for playtime. Once everyone is home and the surroundings are relatively quiet, you can supervise your pet more easily without distractions. Let him roam free in his designated room while you keep a watchful eye, and offer him a variety of toys he can play with and explore such as climbing ladders, tubes, or wheels.

Chinchillas are fun to watch while they play in their cage. However, part

Activity Zones

Because chinchillas are naturally playful and energetic, they will need some sort of activity to help them burn off energy and stay entertained. You can construct special toys that they can use when they are outside their quarters. A series of climbing frames or ladders that run across the floor are highly favoured. Or you could put a large enclosed wheel in an area of the room that is designated as a special play space. Exploring ceramic flowerpots and tubes also appeals to chins. Obviously, out in the open there is more space for activity toys of this type.

Chinchillas relish the opportunity to play in a large interconnected play area. Aside from providing a good opportunity for interactions between you and your pet, activity zones enable you to enjoy watching your pet exercise and play with his favourite toys.

Try to establish a regular schedule for exercise outside the cage.

of the fun of owning them is taking them out of their cage to play. The more you interact with your pet, the happier and friendlier he will be.

Returning Your Chinchilla to His Quarters

After exploring the room, playing, and sitting with you, your chinchilla will ultimately need to be returned to his quarters. This can be difficult in the case of an individual who is not tame simply because he will be harder to catch in more spacious surroundings.

The worse thing to do is to chase around wildly after your chinchilla,

partly because he will find it quite easy to escape your grasp under a piece of furniture in the room. There is also the risk that your pet could become extremely stressed and might even develop heatstroke if you persist in trying to catch him in this way. A calmer, more subtle approach is required, and probably the help of another person.

First, you'll need to decide which corner of the room will be the easiest and most accessible area to catch your pet. Working together from different angles, you must try to guide him to this spot while aiming to block off any possible escape route that might allow him to turn around and slip past you. Crouching down on your hands and knees as you move forward to catch him may save critical seconds, increasing the likelihood that you will reach him and he will not be able to elude your grasp.

As mentioned earlier, aim to place your hand over your pet's back to slow him down, and then scoop him up with your other hand. Never restrain him by his ears or by grabbing at his tail. If your chinchilla struggles, he could experience a serious injury, possibly even stripping the fur off the tail. Any rough handling will result in loss of fur.

The Expert Knows

Litter Training?

Unfortunately, it is not possible to litter train chinchillas in the same way as some other pets, and this means that they may occasionally soil a room when they are let out. Their urinary output is very small, however, and their droppings are quite firm and easy to clean up. There are special pet disinfectants that you can obtain to ensure that the area is thoroughly clean. It obviously helps if you can let your chinchilla scamper around on a tiled floor because it can be disinfected easily when necessary.

Be patient if catching your chinchilla proves difficult, and stop if necessary so that you can rearrange the furniture in the room to make this task easier. The aim is to steer him down a path that has no escape route at the end. Never shout at your chinchilla or scold him if he's not cooperating. This is simply a reflection of his natural instinct to avoid danger.

How Chinchillas Behave

Your chinchilla displays a variety of behaviours in response to different stimuli. Recognising and understanding his vocalisations, body language, and behaviour will help you tame and train him.

Vocalisations

You will realise that your efforts to bond with your chinchilla are proving successful when he responds to you by uttering a quiet squeak. This chortling call reflects his desire to interact with you, and the sound is likely to be heard with increased frequency once he is used to being let out of his quarters at a set time each evening. If ignored, this call is likely to be repeated with increasing frequency as your chinchilla demands your attention.

If a cat comes to sit on your chin's cage or patrols menacingly around the sides of it, expect him to alert you with a warning call. Much louder and insistent in nature, it reflects the danger inherent in the situation. If your chinchilla is in pain for any reason, he will cry out even more loudly. Should he be in an aggressive mood, particularly when confronted by another chinchilla, he will make a growling sound, which serves as a warning. If you suspect that they may not be getting along well together, this will be a firm indicator because it is likely that one of them is being bullied by the other.

When two chinchillas live together, you are likely to be able to pick out their individual vocalisations quite easily with experience because their calls, even with the same meaning, will sound different.

Body Language

You can tell much about your chinchilla's state of mind by his body language. When relaxed and moving slowly around his quarters, a chinchilla will use his short front legs to help him move on all fours. Out in a room, however, where there is more space available, chinchillas are more likely to hop along using their powerful hind legs, with their tail helping them stay upright. The importance of the tail as far as the chinchilla's ability to balance is concerned is especially apparent when he is obtaining an overview of the world around him. At this stage, he will stand up on his hind legs, looking around and sniffing the air while almost balancing backward on his tail.

Chinchillas will often groom themselves using their front paws. This is a sign that all is well and that the animal is quite relaxed. They are generally keen to investigate new objects, but if they are slightly uncertain, they will keep their ears lower, flattening them down toward the back rather than keeping them raised as is usual.

Problem Behaviour

Chinchillas do not generally suffer from many behavioural difficulties, although, as discussed earlier, fur chewing can be a problem. Their most unpleasant trait is the way that they will react if badly frightened, although such behaviour is really only likely to be seen in domesticated chinchillas who are not used to being handled. Nevertheless, if you try to introduce your chinchilla to another individual and they take a dislike to each other, your established pet's natural instincts may take over. He will then stand up on his hind legs and spurt out a jet of urine that is targeted in the direction of the other pet.

Getting Along With Other Pets

Chinchillas do not like being in close proximity to other larger animals. If you already have a cat, supervise your pets closely. Your chinchilla could otherwise be in real danger, depending on the spacing of the bars of his cage. Even if your cat cannot reach the

Monitor all interactions with other household pets so they don't obtain access to your chinchilla.

chinchilla easily, she might still be able to inflict a serious and even potentially fatal injury. This is because a cat's mouth is full of unpleasant bacteria. Following a bite from the long curved teeth at the corner of the cat's jaws, these bacteria are effectively injected deep within the chinchilla's tissue, where they can cause an infection that may spread rapidly throughout the body. Bite wounds need veterinary treatment. Even if your cat simply claws at the chinchilla, it is likely to be serious, particularly if the rodent's vulnerable eyes or ears are injured.

Aside from keeping these pets apart, you also need to make it difficult for your cat to reach your chinchilla by the way in which you position the cage. Try to avoid locating it where it would be easy for your cat to jump up alongside it or hop across from a chair to reach it. It is also very important to reinforce the door closure as further protection. Use a small combination lock that can be opened easily without keys. Depending on the setup in your room, you may want to put up a shelf for your chinchilla, but make sure that it isn't close to a radiator. By placing the cage on a high shelf, it will be impossible for your cat to reach your chinchilla easily.

The way in which a cat will react to the introduction of a chinchilla to the household is likely to vary, depending partly on the age of the cat and also her background. Some types of cat often show more determined hunting instincts than others. Whereas longhaired Persians are rarely interested in exerting themselves, Siamese and other Orientals will frequently try to hunt, being aided by their greater agility.

Young cats are likely to be much more enthusiastic about preying on a chinchilla than an older individual. Nevertheless, don't take any chances because an older cat will still retain her hunting instincts, particularly if there is an easy opportunity to reach him. It is especially important to keep your cat out of the room when you allow your chinchilla out of his quarters.

By contrast, most dogs are not particularly concerned about the addition of a chinchilla to the home, although their barking could upset a chinchilla in his new surroundings if he has not encountered them before.

However, there is a serious risk if your dog manages to get into the room where your chinchilla is being allowed to run free out of his cage. Many dogs, but particularly those of terrier or hound breeds, may instinctively give chase. You'll have to hope that your chinchilla manages to scamper up on to a shelf because the dog will not be able to climb up there.

If you keep a pet like a house rabbit, she probably won't upset your chinchilla, although you'll need to be certain that he will not be able to steal the rabbit's food if they are both out of the cage at the same time. Parrots or other birds are also likely

Carrier Training

Because chinchillas normally frequent darkened surroundings, they are unlikely to be disturbed by being kept in the semi-darkness of a travel carrier. Provided that there is some clean bedding inside, they will usually settle down quite readily. The simplest way to accustom your pet to this environment is to place him in the carrier whenever you are cleaning out his quarters.

Finger Nipping

Children really enjoy playing with chinchillas and rewarding them with treats for good behaviour. But do not encourage a child to place a finger through the sides of the chinchilla's cage because this will almost inevitably result in a bite. This is not likely to be serious, though, because chinchillas use their teeth combined with their sense of taste to determine whether something is edible by testing it gently. It could, however, be a problem if you are holding a small treat like a raisin because fingers are at much greater risk of being badly bitten in this case.

to ignore a chinchilla, but be sure that your chinchilla cannot run across the parrot's quarters or clamber up the sides when out of his own cage. Otherwise, the bird may respond by snapping at the rodent's toes and could inflict a serious bite. Most herps will ignore a chinchilla, but beware with snakes because rodents are the natural prey of many species.

Should you have an aquarium, you must keep it properly covered with a hood to prevent your chinchilla from gaining access. Even if he does not tumble down into the water, simply drinking aquarium water may be harmful because it contains a much higher number of potentially harmful microbes than ordinary tap water.

Arranging for Care

It will be important for other members of the family and several of your friends to build up a bond with your chinchilla, particularly because there

may be times when they will need to care for your pet.

You are most likely to need the assistance of another adult member of the household or a friend to look after your pet when you go out of town. Unfortunately, chinchillas do not enjoy being moved, so taking your pet with you when you go on vacation is not a good idea, even if you are not going to be away for very long or travelling very far. The stress of the journey is likely to be upsetting, and the risk of digestive upsets as well as heatstroke will both be significantly increased out on the road.

You will therefore need to show your friend just what will be entailed in looking after your chinchilla in your absence. It may help to print out a daily checklist explaining what needs to be done, especially if the person concerned has never kept a chinchilla before. If you must leave your pet with someone, try to choose a friend who does not have a cat. It also will be safer if your chinchilla is not let out in strange surroundings because of the risk of accidents.

Children are often keen to be involved in petsitting, but be careful that your chinchilla is not overwhelmed with constant attention or handling during these situations. He will need some time to settle down and become familiar with his new surroundings. Too much stroking will not only stress him but may even affect his fur, causing it to flatten. The age of the children taking care of your pet will directly affect the extent to which they can become involved in his care. The important thing is to be sure that they are always supervised and properly instructed in your pet's daily needs. Of course, you want to be sure that they have had enough experience with caring for your pet before assigning him to their care while you are away.

When planning for your pet's care, it's always best to opt for having him looked after in your own home because this will cause the least amount of stress. Also, be sure to have enough pet supplies on hand, as well as contact numbers for your vet and for yourself in case of an emergency.

For a Lifetime

Bringing a pet into your home means a period of adjustment while he gets used to you and you get used to having him around too. Your chinchilla's proper care and well-being represent a commitment you made to him for his entire lifetime. Taking the time to understand him and all of his behaviours and needs will allow you to build a bond of trust that will enrich your experience together.

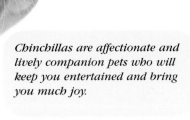

Chinchillas are affectionate and lively companion pets who will keep you entertained and bring you much joy.

Glossary

agouti—The alternating light and dark bands extending down each hair, which is the natural patterning of wild chinchillas.

albino—A pure white individual lacking any colour pigment so the eyes are reddish and the skin is pale.

alfalfa—A plant used as a food source for chinchillas, usually being provided in the form of hay.

ano-genital gap/space—The area between the opening of the anus and the genitals, which is used as a means of determining the gender of young chinchillas, being longer in males than in females.

antibiotics—Types of medication used to combat bacterial infections, which may be administered in various ways such as by injection or in the form of ointment.

bale—A large bag of wood shavings used as cage bedding.

breeder—A person who keeps chinchillas and breeds them, often selling surplus stock as pets.

cataract—A whitish area that may become evident on the eyes of older chinchillas that reflects a deterioration in their vision.

carrier— A small container suitable for moving a chinchilla. Also describes a chinchilla carrying a particular colour in its genes, which may emerge later in its offspring.

caviomorph—Chinchillas and other rodents such as guinea pigs and degus are part of this family. Characteristics of the group include young being born in an advanced state of development after a relatively long gestation period, with the number of offspring in a litter being quite small.

cardon— A terrestrial bromeliad plant favoured by chinchillas.

caecum—An enlarged part of the digestive tract located between the small and large intestines, where a population of beneficial microbes aid the breakdown of plant matter in the chinchilla's diet.

chin—An abbreviated form of "chinchilla", sometimes affectionately used by breeders and pet owners alike.

chinchilla bath—The container used to provide the dust for bathing purposes.

chinchilla dust—A special product that helps to keep a chinchilla's coat in top condition.

Chinchilla brevicaudata—The species of chinchilla known as the short-tailed chinchilla.

Chinchilla lanigera—The scientific name for the long-tailed chinchilla, which is the ancestor of today's pet chinchillas.

chromosome—The microscopic, threadlike structures within the nucleus of all cells, usually occurring in pairs, that carry all the individual's characteristics.

colony—A group of individuals living together.

crepuscular—Becoming active at dusk.

cusps—The raised areas on the chinchilla's molar teeth.

dilute colouration— A change in a chinchilla's appearance, as the result of a mutation, so that it appears paler than normal.

exercise wheel—A broad, solid wheel with a flat edge that allows chinchillas to exercise in their quarters.

exotics veterinarian—A veterinarian whose main interest is the treatment of chinchillas and other rodents, as well as other small pets and herps.

fancy—The selective breeding of colour variants for their appearance.

gene—The area of a chromosome where information about the individual's inherited characteristics are stored.

gestation—The period following mating, from conception through birth.

hay cubes—Compressed hay given to chinchillas.

heatstroke—A condition to which chinchillas are vulnerable, caused by being kept in surroundings that are too hot.

hormones—Chemical messengers produced in one part of the body that are then carried to another in the blood; these act to produce a specific often stimulatory effect on the activity of cells usually remote from their point of origin.

ideal—The desired appearance of an exhibition chinchilla of a particular variety.

incisors—The two long front teeth present in the centre of the top and bottom jaws.

independent—The stage at which a young chinchilla is feeding adequately on his own and can be separated from his mother.

kit—The name used to describe a young chinchilla.

lactation—The period during which a female chinchilla produces milk for her offspring, under hormonal control.

malocclusion—A deviation of the incisor teeth, which may be inherited or the result of an accident, causing them to become overgrown to the extent they will need trimming back regularly so the chinchilla can eat.

mammal—An animal able to regulate its body temperature independently of its environment, with hair on its body. The young are suckled by the female.

molars—The so-called "cheek teeth" present at the back of the chinchilla's mouth.

moult—The way in which hairs are shed from the coat, usually as part of a regular seasonal pattern.

mosaic—A pied form of the chinchilla, with white and dark-coloured areas in the coat.

mutation—A change in the chinchilla's appearance, usually describing his colouration, that can be passed on from one generation to the next, although it may not always be visible in the appearance of littermates.

myomorphs—The largest group within the rodent family, which includes mice and rats. The young are born after a short gestation period in a immature state of development.

nestbox—Sleeping area made of wood provided for the chinchillas, sometimes also described as the den.

nocturnal—The behaviour of an animal such as a chinchilla that tends to sleep during the day and then wakes up around nightfall.

normal—Typical colouration associated with that species, as reflected by the standard.

parasite—Another organism that, depending on its type, may live on or in another (called the host), causing harm.

pastel—A dark beige form of the chinchilla.

pearl—A light beige form of the chinchilla.

pedigree—The ancestry of the animal extending back over several generations.

pellets—Commercially-produced food containing all the key nutrients that chinchillas require to keep them healthy.

pelt—The name given to the chinchilla's coat in the fur industry.

points—Refers to the extremities of the body, such as the ears, face, legs, feet, and tail that may differ in colour, sometimes being a darker shade than the body itself.

probiotic—A product containing beneficial bacteria that may aid the recovery of a sick chinchilla after antibiotic treatment.

priming line—The line that moves through the coat, indicating how the chinchilla is moulting.

ranch chinchillas—Chinchillas being kept for their fur.

rancher—A person who breeds chinchillas for their fur, rather than as pets.

rehoming—The process of finding a new home for a chinchilla whose previous owner is unable or unwilling to care properly for their pet.

rescue organisation/group—An organisation that seeks to ensure the welfare of chinchillas. It also acts in the case of those that may be neglected and is often engaged in rehoming.

ringworm—A fungal infection that can be spread between chinchillas and people causing circular patches of hair loss in chinchillas and relatively large, red circular patches on the skin.

shed—An alternative word for "moult" describing the way in which hair is lost from the coat, usually on a regular basis.

rodent—Belonging to the order Rodentia, which is the largest division of mammals, representing some 1,700 species, equivalent to 40 percent of the world's total.

self—An individual displaying a single colour on his coat.

senior—An elderly chinchilla, probably over about 8 years of age.

show standard—The scale of points to which chinchillas may be judged at shows.

solid food—The type of food eaten by chinchillas once they are fully weaned.

species—Animals that display a close relationship to each other, usually occurring in the same area.

spot cleaning—The way in which evident soiling is removed from the chinchilla's quarters.

spur—An overgrowth on a chinchilla's molar teeth that is likely to make eating difficult.

styptic—A means of stemming minor blood flow.

subspecies—A subdivision of species, being used to describe two populations of the same species that differ slightly in appearance from each other.

standard—The name given to the colouration seen in wild chinchillas.

timothy—A form of grass used as chinchilla food.

type—The characteristic appearance associated with a show specimen. May be deemed either good or poor.

variety—A variant; a term typically used to describe a colour form of the chinchilla.

veiling—The way in which the chinchilla's main colouration envelops his body.

water bottle—A secure means of providing fresh, clean drinking water for chinchillas; a bottle attached to the sides of the living quarters.

weaning—The stage at which a young chinchillas becomes progressively less dependent on his mother's milk and starts to eat solid food instead.

whiskers—The prominent, thick, spacialised hairs evident on the chinchilla's head that help him to find his way around, particularly after dark or in underground burrows.

zoonosis—A disease that can be transmitted from an animal to a person (and vice versa), the plural of which is zoonoses.

Resources

Clubs and Societies

National Chinchilla Society
101 Simmondley Lane,
Glossop, Derbyshire SK13 6LU.
Telephone: 01457-856945
E-mail: chillaquip@freeuk.com
www.natchinsoc.co.uk

The Chinchilla Club
(The International Pet Chinchilla
Organisation)
E-mail: info@chinclub.net
www.chinclub.net

Animal Welfare Groups and Adoption Organisations

Royal Society for the Prevention of
Cruelty to Animals (RSPCA)
Telephone: 0870 3335 999
Fax: 0870 7530 284
www.rspca.org.uk

Scottish Society for the Prevention of
Cruelty to Animals (SSPCA) Braehead
Mains
603 Queensferry Road
Edinburgh EH4 6EA
Telephone: 0131 339 0222

British Veterinary Association Animal
Welfare Foundation (BVA AWF)7
Mansfield Street
London W1G 9NQ
Telephone: 0207 636 6541
Email: bva-awf@bva.co.uk
www.bva-awf.org.uk

Pet Rescue UK
www.pet-rescue.org.uk

Chinchillas 4 Life
www.chinchillas4life.co.uk

Chinchilla Rescue Service
C.F.P.N.P Club & Rescue Service
P.O. Box 5583
Nottingham, NG16 5QR
www.chinchilla.co.uk

Chinchilla Rescue
01430-879108
E-mail: chinchillarescue@hotmail.co.uk
www.chinchillarescue.com

Chinchillas

Veterinary and Health Resources

British Veterinary Association (BVA)
7 Mansfield Street
London
W1G 9NQ
Telephone: 020 7636 6541
Fax: 020 7436 2970
E-mail: bvahq@bva.co.uk
www.bva.co.uk

British Small Animal Veterinary
Association (BSAVA)
Woodrow House
1 Telford Way
Waterwells Business Park
Quedgley
Gloucester GL2 2AB
Telephone: 01452 726700
email: customerservices@bsava.com
www.bsava.com

British Association of Homeopathic
Veterinary Surgeons
Alternative Veterinary Medicine Centre
Chinham House
Stanford in the Vale
Oxfordshire
SN7 8NQ
Email: enquiries@bahvs.com
www.bahvs.com

British Veterinary Hospitals Association
(BHVA)
Station Bungalow
Main Road, Stockfield
Northumberland NE43 7HJ
Telephone: 07966 901619
Email: office@bvha.org.uk
www.BVHA.org.uk

PDSA
www.pdsa.org.uk
Head Office
Whitechapel Way
Priorslee
Telford
Shropshire
TF2 9PQ
Telephone: 01952 290999

Pet Care Trust
Bedford Business Centre
170 Mile Road
Bedford
MK42 9TW
Telephone: 01234 273 933
www.petcare.org.uk
E-mail: info@petcare.org.uk

105

Resources

Websites

www.chincare.com
A very extensive list of resources, including lists of veterinarians on a state-by-state basis who are experienced in treating chinchillas. Also includes veterinarians in other countries, such as Canada, the UK, Japan, and Singapore. This site aims to list all the current chinchilla sites in English on the web (as well as other languages) making it the ideal starting point when you are seeking further information on any aspect of chinchillas and their care.

www.chinchillaburg.com
Current attempts to conserve chinchillas in the wild are featured on this site, as well as advice about their care. Available in both German and English.

www.chinchillaworld.com
A very active forum for chinchilla enthusiasts where care tips and other information are discussed. Incorporates special features such as a pregnancy calculator, if you are breeding your chinchillas.

www.chinclub.net.
The Chinchilla Club is an international website catering to all aspects of owning chinchillas. There are even breeder directories to help you find a breeder near you.

www.sleepychinchilla.com
Enjoy watching webcasts that show the exploits of a group of chinchillas living in Bristol. Regularly online, it offers past movies and slideshows as well.

Publications

Magazines

Fur and Feather Magazine
Printing for Pleasure Ltd
Elder House, Chattisham
Ipswich, Suffolk, IP8 3QE
Telephone: 01473 652789
E-mail: info@furandfeather.co.uk

Online Pet Magazine
www.petmag.co.uk

The Chinchilla Community Magazine
http://chinchillamagazine.com/pages/
A publication that has now become
presently available only on-line.
Available to members of either the
Chinchilla Club or Chinchilla Breeders
Organisation.

Books

Page, Gill, *Getting to Know Your Chinchilla*, Interpet Publishing

Poli, Mirella, *An Essential Guide to Owning a Chinchilla*, Kindgom Books

Whear, Roger, *How to Care For Your Chinchilla*, Kingdom Books

Alderton, David, *The Small Animals Question & Answer Manual*, Interpet Publishing.

Barrie, Annmarie, *Guide to Owning a Chinchilla*, TFH Publications, Inc.

Pavia, Audrey, *A New Owner's Guide to Chinchillas*, TFH Publications, Inc.

Roder-Thiede, Maike, *Chinchillas (A Complete Pet Owner's Manual)*, Barrons Educational Series, Inc.

Index

development. *See* behaviour and development

diarrhoea, 14, 41, 69, 71
diet changes, 43–45
digestion, 39–41, 71–72
dogs and chinchillas, 23, 91, 97
domestication of chinchillas, 12
droppings, appearance of, 14
dust bath, 31–32, 55–56, **57**

E

ear care, 61–62
E.coli, 68
emergencies, 76, 105
  broken bones, 79
  cuts and scrapes, 73–74
  escapes, 93–94
  heatstroke, 22, 54, **56**
  illness, signs of, 70
  poisoning, 79–80
  preparation for, 72
  safety issues, 90–92
endangered species, **10**
exercise, 30, 92–93
eye care, 62–63
eye problems, 72–73

F

family groups, 7, 9
fats in diet, 41
feeding
  age appropriate guidelines for, 48
  alfalfa cubes, 46
  amount to feed, 40, 44, 45, 47, 50–51
  carbohydrates, 41
  diet changes, 43–45
  fats, 41
  food dishes and, 29
  fruits, 50–51
  hay, 45–47
  herbs, 48–49
  minerals and vitamins, 42
  nuts and seeds, 47
  pellets for, 43–45
  proteins, 41
  schedule for, 40
  supplements, 43
  treats, 49–51, 86
  twigs and branches, 51
  unhealthy foods, 47

vegetables, 47–48
water and, 29–30, 51
weaning, 14
female vs. male, 15, 19
first aid, 76, 105
  broken bones, 79
  cuts and scrapes, 73–74
  heatstroke, 22, 54, **56**
  illness, signs of, 70
  poisoning, 79–80
  preparation for, 72
  safety issues, 90–92
food dishes, 29
fruits in diet, 50–51
fur
  chewing of, 75–76
  condition of, 57, 74
  loss of, 74–77, 79

G

gender selection, **14**, 19
grooming
  age appropriate guidelines for, 63
  bathing, 31–32, 55–56, **57**
  combing, 54, 55
  dust bath and, 31–32, 55–56, **57**
  ear care, 61–62
  eye care, 62–63
  health checks and, 60
  nail care, 59, 61
  schedule for, 56–57
  supplies for, 55
  teeth trimming, **59**

H

handling, 85, 86–89, 98–99
hay in diet, 45–47
hay rack, 30, 45–46
health issues. *see also* behaviour and development; first aid
  antibiotics, 71–72
  body temperature, 70, 80
  cleanliness, 68
  dental care, 15–16, 31, 57–60
  dermatitis, 28
  diarrhoea, 14, 41, 69, 71
  digestive disorders, 71–72
  droppings, appearance of, 14
  escaped pets, 93–94
  exercise, 30, 92–93

111

Index

About the Author

David Alderton is an international best-selling authority on pets and their care. His books have sold over six million copies in 27 languages worldwide. He has also been published widely in a variety of magazines and broadcasts regularly about animals and natural history on both television and radio.

David's interest in chinchillas began over 25 years ago, when he first saw a pair of them in his local pet shop. He has since gained considerable insight into their behaviour and needs. His resulting expertise has also led to his involvement in training programmes designed for pet shop personnel about the proper care of chinchillas and other small pets. He lives near the city of Brighton in Southern England.